EXCEL 2002

in easy

STEPHEN COPESTAKE

In easy steps is an imprint of Computer Step
Southfield Road . Southam
Warwickshire CV47 0FB . England

http://www.ineasysteps.com

Notice of Liability

Every effort has been made to ensure that this book contains accurate and current information. However, Computer Step and the author shall not be liable for any loss or damage suffered by readers as a result of any information contained herein.

Trademarks

Microsoft® and Windows® are registered trademarks of Microsoft Corporation. All other trademarks are acknowledged as belonging to their respective companies.

Printed and bound in the United Kingdom

ISBN 1-84078-142-4

Table of Contents

Getting started

This chapter shows you how to get started quickly in Excel 2002. You'll learn about its screen and the terminology it uses, then work with toolbars and enter/handwrite data. You'll navigate through worksheets and use Ask-a-Question to find specific help. Finally, you'll enhance your use of Excel with additional features (these include Quick File Switching, error repair, copying/pasting multiple items, using the Task Pane and signing documents digitally).

Covers

Chapter One

The Excel 2002 screen

Below is a detailed illustration of the Excel 2002 screen:

Title bar   Menu bar   Column letters

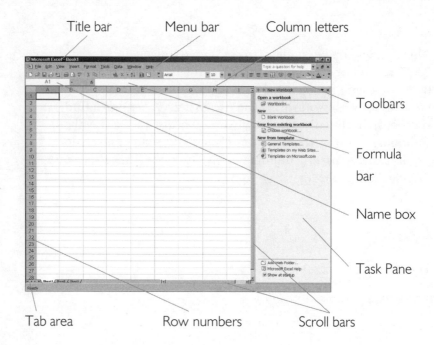

Toolbars

Formula
bar

Name box

Task Pane

Tab area   Row numbers   Scroll bars

Some of these screen components can be hidden at will.

Specifying which screen components display

Pull down the Tools menu and click Options. Then:

Click View

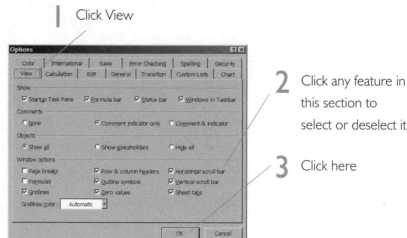

2 Click any feature in
this section to
select or deselect it

3 Click here

*You can use a
special wizard
– the Save My
Settings
Wizard – to
save configuration details in
a special file (with the
extension .ops). You can
then restore the details in
the file as a way of
transferring your Excel (and
any other Office module)
settings to another machine,
or as a backup for your
existing PC.*

*First close Excel and any
other Office programs. Click
Start, Programs, Microsoft
Office Tools, Save My
Settings Wizard. Follow the
on-screen instructions.*

Screen components in detail

Cells occur where rows and columns intersect.

Components shown in the opening screen on page 8 are explained in more detail now:

The worksheet

This is the large central rectangular area which is subdivided into a grid of cells. The cells are used to store data.

Note that the Excel 2002 Control menu looks like this:

The Title Bar

The Title Bar contains the program title and the name of the overall Excel workbook. It also contains (at the left-hand end) the button for the pull-down Control menu:

One way to close Excel 2002 is to double-click this button with the left-hand mouse button.

The Menu Bar

This contains menu titles for all the commands used to build, format and control Excel worksheets. Clicking any title with the left mouse button will display a pull-down menu from which various options may be selected.

For a more detailed definition of worksheets and workbooks, see

page 13.

Toolbars

Toolbars are collections of icons representing the most commonly used commands required for standard tasks. By clicking an icon, you initiate the command. This represents a major saving in time and effort.

Excel 2002 comes with almost 20 toolbars, of which perhaps the most commonly used are:

Menus and toolbars are also self-customising – see pages

11-12.

- Standard

- Formatting

- Web

See pages 10–12 for how to customise and work with toolbars.

For how to use the vertical and horizontal scroll bars to navigate through Excel 2002 worksheets, see page 20.

To create your own toolbar, pull down the Tools menu and click Customize. In the Customize dialog, select the Toolbars tab. Click New. In the Toolbar name: field in the New Toolbar dialog, name the new toolbar. Click OK.

(To add buttons to your new toolbar, follow the procedures on page 11.)

The Formula Bar

This displays the location and contents of the currently selected cell. The Formula Bar represents a particularly useful way to enter:

- formulas

- other cell data (e.g. text)

Column headings

Column headings define each cell within a given column horizontally. Columns are labelled A, B, C, etc.

Row headings

Row headings define each cell within a given row vertically. Rows are numbered 1, 2, 3, etc.

The Vertical Scroll Bar

This enables you to move the visible window vertically up and down the worksheet, under the control of the mouse.

The Horizontal Scroll Bar

This enables you to move the visible window horizontally to the left or right across the worksheet.

Sheet tabs

These enable you to select which spreadsheet should be displayed. By clicking on a sheet tab, you jump to the relevant sheet.

(You can also use sheet tabs to perform operations on more than one worksheet at a time.)

The Task Pane

The Task Pane is a specialised task-based toolbar – see page 30.

Working with toolbars

To strip the screen so it contains only the Menu bar and Row/ Column headings (a technique which makes it easier to work with large worksheets), pull down the View menu and click Full Screen.

To return to the normal view, do the following:

Click here

Toolbars are important components in Excel 2002. A toolbar is an on-screen bar which contains shortcut buttons. These symbolise and allow easy access to often-used commands which would normally have to be invoked via one or more menus.

For example, Excel 2002's Standard toolbar lets you:

- create, open, save and print documents

- perform copy & paste and cut & paste operations

- undo editing actions

- access Excel's HELP system

by simply clicking on the relevant button.

You can control which toolbars display.

Specifying which toolbars are visible

Pull down the View menu and click Toolbars. Now do the following:

To add a new button to a toolbar, right-click over the toolbar. Click Customize. In the dialog which launches, click the Commands tab. In the Categories field, click a category (a group of associated icons). In the Commands box, drag a button onto the toolbar in the open document. Finally, click Close.

The Task Pane is a toolbar. To hide or show it, untick or tick the Task Pane entry.

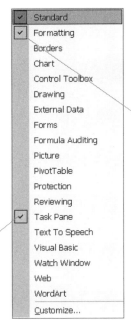

Click the toolbar you want to make visible – a ✔ appears against it

Repeat this procedure for as many toolbars as necessary.

Automatic customisation

As you use Excel 2002, individual features are dynamically promoted or demoted in the relevant menus.
  This means menus are continually evolving...

Until Excel 2000, it was true that, although different users use different features, no allowance had been made for this: the same features displayed on everyone's menus and toolbars...

Now, however, menus and toolbars are personalised.

Personalised menus

When you first use Excel, its menus display the features which Microsoft believes are used 95% of the time. Features which are infrequently used are not immediately visible. This is made clear in the illustrations below:

Menus expand automatically. Simply pull down the required menu, (which will at first be abbreviated) then wait a few seconds: it expands to display the full menu.
  However, to expand them manually, click here on the chevrons at the bottom of the menu.

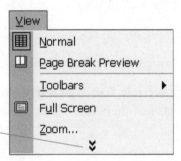

Excel 2002's View menu, as it first appears...

Automatic customisation also applies to toolbars. Note the following:

- *if possible, they display on a single row*
- *they overlap when there isn't enough room on-screen*
- *icons are 'promoted' and 'demoted' like menu entries*
- *demoted icons are shown in a separate fly-out, reached by clicking:*

...the expanded menu

Basic terminology

Here, we explore some of the basic terms used throughout Excel 2002.

Worksheets

'Worksheet' is Excel's name for a spreadsheet. Worksheets are arrays of cells used to store data. This often involves simple arithmetical calculations linking the cells together in tables, usually for some kind of analysis.

By default, Excel workbooks contain 3 worksheets:

- *Sheet 1*
- *Sheet 2*
- *Sheet 3*

Worksheets are the essential building-blocks of workbooks – see below.

Workbooks

A workbook is a file which holds together a collection of worksheets (and possibly charts – for more information on charts, see Chapter 15). It will be seen in later chapters that it is usual to have several worksheets linked together and often convenient to summarise the data on these worksheets in the form of associated charts or graphs.

See Chapter 4 for more information on workbooks.

When you create a new document in Excel, you're actually creating a new workbook. Each new workbook has a default name: Book 1, Book 2 etc.

The Worksheet Window

The opening Excel 2002 window displays (if the Task Pane is not visible):

- 12 columns labelled A to L

- 28 rows labelled 1 to 28

The exact number of rows and columns shown depends on the screen size, video driver and resolution.

It must be appreciated that this is only the extreme top left-hand corner of the full worksheet which extends to:

This means each worksheet contains 16,777,216 cells.

- 256 columns labelled A to Z then AA to IV

- 65,536 rows labelled 1 to 65,536

See the illustration on page 14 for further clarification.

As we've just seen, the Excel 2002 screen displays only a tiny section of the available worksheet. The illustration below displays this graphically:

This area covers the cell range A1 to I18.

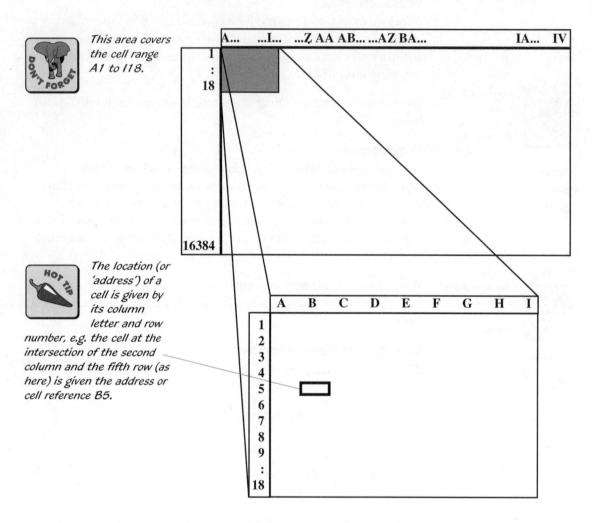

The location (or 'address') of a cell is given by its column letter and row number, e.g. the cell at the intersection of the second column and the fifth row (as here) is given the address or cell reference B5.

The grey section – only a tiny part of the overall worksheet – is shown in its overall context in the lower half of the illustration.

Keying in data

In Excel 2002, you can enter the following basic data types:

- values (i.e. numbers)

- text (e.g. headings and explanatory material)

- functions (e.g. Sine or Cosine)

- formulas (combinations of values, text and functions)

You can use two techniques to enter data into any cell in a worksheet.

Entering data directly

First, move the mouse pointer over any cell and left-click once. Alternatively, you can also use the keyboard to target a cell: simply move the cell pointer with the cursor keys until it's over the relevant cell.

Whichever method you use, Excel 2002 surrounds the active cell with a border.

Excel 2002 lets you insert and work with Euros. To insert the Euro symbol, hold down Alt and type 0128 on the Numerical keypad to the right of your keyboard. Finally, release Alt.

The principal fonts that currently support the Euro are:

- *Courier*
- *Tahoma*
- *Times*
- *Arial*

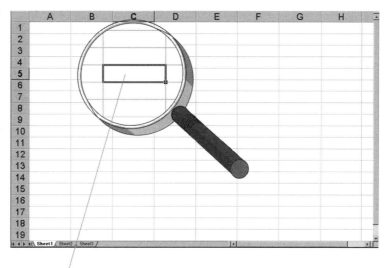

Magnified view of active cell

Now begin to key in the information required. It will appear simultaneously in the cell and in the Formula Bar.

When you enter values which are too big (physically) to fit in the holding cell, Excel 2002 may insert an error message.

To resolve this, pull down the Format menu and click Column, AutoFit Selection to have Excel 2002 automatically increase the column size to match the contents.

... and in the Formula bar

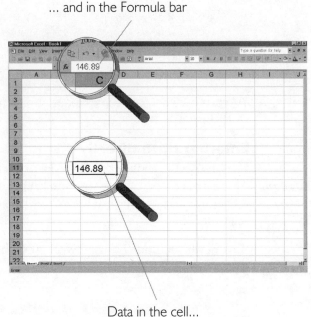

Data in the cell...

Finally, press Enter to confirm entry of the data (or Esc to cancel the operation).

Entering data via the Formula bar

You can use a keyboard route to confirm operations in the Formula bar: simply press Enter.

Click the cell you want to insert data into. Then click the Formula Bar. Type in the data. Then follow step 1 below. If you decide not to proceed with the operation, follow step 2 instead:

1 Click here

2 Click here

Handwriting data

You can handwrite data into a special writing pad and have Excel convert it into standard text. You can also use a virtual keyboard to enter text.

1 If the Language Bar isn't visible or minimised on the Taskbar, go to Control Panel. Double-click Text Services. In the dialog, click Language Bar. Select Show the Language bar on the desktop. Click OK twice

2 Click Handwriting

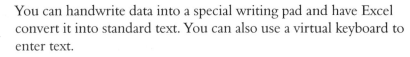

Language Bar

3 Select Writing Pad

4 Handwrite data on the line in the Writing Pad (don't pause between letters/digits but do leave appropriate spaces) – Excel enters the data as soon as it recognizes it

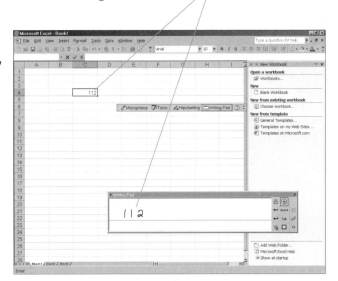

Selection techniques

Excel 2002 uses See-Through Selection – selected cells (except the first) are lightly shaded, so that you can see the result of any changes you make to underlying data.

Before you can carry out any editing operations on cells in Excel 2002, you have to select them first. Selecting a single cell is very easy: you merely click in it (we examined this on page 15). However, Excel provides a variety of selection techniques which you can use to select more than one cell.

1.   Selecting adjacent cell ranges

The easiest way to do this is to use the mouse. Click in the first cell in the range; hold down the left mouse button and drag over the remaining cells. Release the mouse button.

You can use the keyboard, too. Select the first cell in the range. Hold down one Shift key as you use the relevant cursor key to extend the selection. Release the keys when the correct selection has been defined.

Re 1. – you can use another keyboard route. Place the cell pointer in the first cell. Press F8 – the following appears in the Status bar at the base of the screen:

2.   Selecting separate cell ranges

Excel lets you select more than one range at a time. Look at the illustration below:

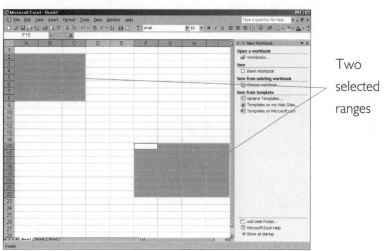

Two selected ranges

Shows that Excel is in Selection mode

Use the cursor keys to define the selection. Finally, press F8 again.

To select joint ranges, select the first in the normal way (you can only use the mouse method here). Then hold down Ctrl as you select subsequent ranges.

Groups of adjacent cells are known as 'ranges' in Excel. Ranges are described in terms of their upper-left and lower-right cell references (with each separated by a colon).

For example, the range beginning with cell D3 and ending with H16 would be shown as:

D3:H16

3. Selecting a single row or column

To select every cell within a row or column automatically, click the row or column heading.

Column heading

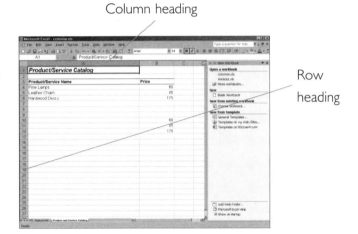

Row heading

4. Selecting multiple rows or columns

Note that non-adjacent ranges are separated by commas e.g.:

A3:B9,D3:H16

To select more than one row or column, click a row or column heading. Hold down the left mouse button and drag to select adjacent rows or columns.

5. Selecting an entire worksheet

Carry out step 1 below:

Click the Select All button

You can use a keyboard shortcut to select every cell automatically. Simply press Ctrl+A.

Moving around in worksheets

Excel 2002 worksheets are huge. Moving to cells which happen to be visible is easy: you simply click in the relevant cell. However, Excel provides several techniques you can use to jump to less accessible areas.

Using the scroll bars

Use any of the following methods:

1. to scroll quickly to another section of the active worksheet, drag the scroll box along the scroll bar until you reach it

2. to move one window to the right or left, click to the left or right of the scroll box in the horizontal scroll bar

3. to move one window up or down, click above or below the scroll box in the vertical scroll bar

4. to move up or down by one row, click the arrows in the vertical scroll bar

5. to move left or right by one column, click the arrows in the horizontal scroll bar

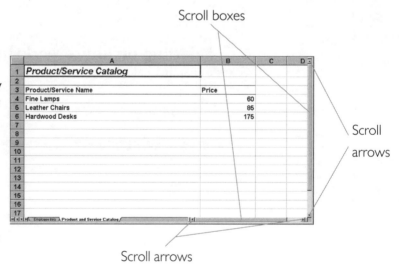

Scroll boxes

Scroll arrows

Scroll arrows

Switching between worksheets

See page 8 if you're not sure how to find the Tab area.

Because workbooks have more than one worksheet, Excel 2002 provides two easy and convenient methods for moving between them.

Using the Tab area

You can use the Tab area (at the base of the Excel screen) to:

- jump to the first or last sheet

- jump to the next or previous sheet

- jump to a specific sheet

See the illustration below:

When you click a worksheet tab, Excel 2002 emboldens the name and makes the tab background white.

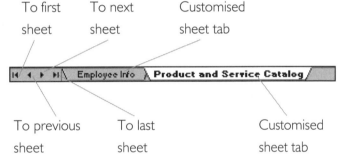

You can 'colour-code' worksheet tabs, for ease of reference.
Right-click a tab and select Tab Color in the shortcut menu. Select a colour and click OK.

To move to a specific sheet, simply click the relevant tab.

An example: in the illustration above, to jump to the 'Employee Info' worksheet, simply click the appropriate tab.

Using the keyboard

You can use keyboard shortcuts here:

You can use the Go To dialog to move to a cell's 'reference' or 'address' (they identify it in relation to its position in a worksheet).
Press F5. In the Reference field, type in a reference (e.g. H12) or a range (e.g. J25:K36). Click OK.

Ctrl+Page Up	moves to the previous tab/sheet
Ctrl+Page Down	moves to the next tab/sheet

Using the Watch Window

Excel provides a special toolbar called the Watch Window. As the name implies, you can use this to track cells (usually those containing formulas) while you're working on another part of the same worksheet, or another worksheet or workbook.

Launching the Watch Window

1 Right-click the cell you want to track

2 Click here

3 The cell has been added to the Watch Window

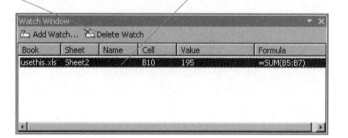

4 To call up the Watch Window when you don't want to add or remove cells, pull down the Tools menu and click Formula Auditing, Watch Window

Using Excel 2002's HELP system

Excel supports the standard Windows HELP system. For instance:

- Moving the mouse pointer over toolbar buttons produces an explanatory HELP bubble:

- You can move the mouse pointer over fields in dialogs, commands or screen areas and produce a specific HELP box. Carry out the following procedure to achieve this:

Excel 2002 calls these highly specific HELP bubbles 'ScreenTips'.

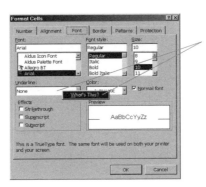

Right-clicking a field and left-clicking the box which launches...

Select an underline type to format the selected text with an underline.

...produces a specific HELP topic

Other standard Windows HELP features are also present; see your Windows documentation for how to use these. Additionally, Excel 2002 has inbuilt HELP in the normal way...

Ask-a-Question

In Excel 2000, users had to run the Office Assistant (see the tip) to get answers to plain-English questions. In Excel 2002, however, this isn't the case. Simply do the following:

The Office Assistant is turned off by default. To turn it on, pull down the Help menu and click Show Office Assistant.

The Assistant is an animated (and frequently unpopular) helper which answers questions, but you can achieve the same effect more easily with Ask-a-Question.

Type in your question here and press Enter

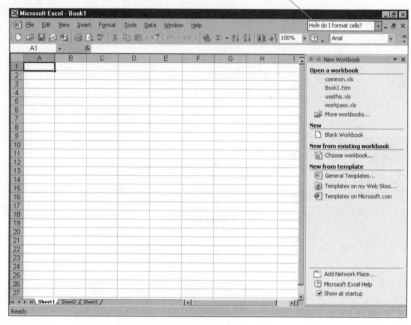

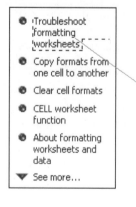

2 Click a relevant entry (or See more, for more topics)

3 Optional – click Show All to display all sub-topics

Use the Contents and Index tabs as you would in any other

program. *program.*

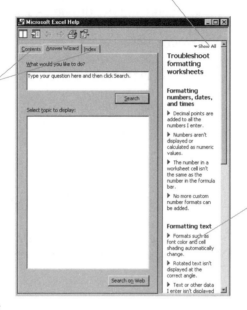

4 Or click an individual topic

To print out a topic, click this icon:

The result of step 3 – all the topics are enlarged (the expanded text is shown in green)

Quick File Switching

In order to use Quick File Switching you need to be using:

- *Windows 98/2000/Me, or later:*
- *Windows 95 with Internet Explorer 4.0 (or a later version)*

In the past, only programs (not individual windows within programs) displayed on the Windows Taskbar. With Excel 2002, however, all open windows display as separate buttons.

In the following example, four new documents have been created in Excel 2002. All four display as separate windows, although only one copy of Excel 2002 is running:

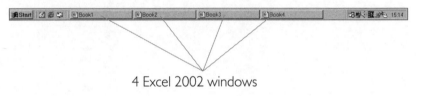

4 Excel 2002 windows

To begin a discussion (see the HOT TIP on page 27 for how to pre-select a server), open a workbook. Pull down the Tools menu and click Online Collaboration, Web Discussions. Click the Discussions button in the toolbar at the base of the screen; select Insert about the Workbook. Follow the on-screen instructions.

This is clarified by a glance at Excel 2002's Window menu which (as with previous versions) shows all open Excel windows:

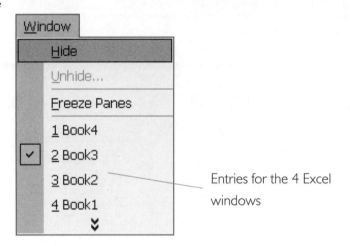

Entries for the 4 Excel windows

Use this technique to go to a workbook window by simply clicking its Taskbar button – a considerable saving in time and effort.

Repairing errors

If Office Server Extensions have been installed on a Web server, you can add discussions to Excel documents (inc. HTML files) stored on it.

Open a workbook/ worksheet. Ensure your Internet connection is live. Pull down the Tools menu and click Online Collaboration, Web Discussions. The Discussion Options dialog appears. (If it doesn't, click the Discussions button in the toolbar at the base of the screen and select Discussion Options in the menu.)

Click Add. Follow the on-screen instructions.

Excel 2002 provides a special feature you can use for damage repair.

Detect and Repair

Do the following to correct program errors (but note selecting Discard my customised settings and restore default settings in step 2 will ensure that all default Excel settings are restored, so any you've customised – including menu/toolbar position and view settings – will be lost):

1 Pull down the Help menu and select Detect and Repair

2 Select one or both options

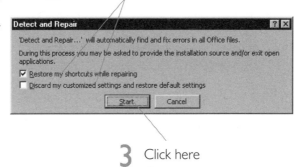

3 Click here

4 Follow the on-screen instructions – Detect and Repair can be a lengthy process

5 You may have to re-enter your user name and initials when you restart your Office applications

You can use another method to repair damaged files. Press Ctrl+O. In the open dialog, highlight the corrupt file and click the drop-down arrow on the Open button. In the menu, click Open and Repair.

(Excel may run this procedure automatically when errors are detected.)

...cont'd

You can also use a further procedure for instances when Excel 'hangs' (ceases to respond).

Application Recovery

When errors occur, Excel should give you the option of saving open files before the application closes.

1 Click Start, Programs, Microsoft Office Tools, Microsoft Office Application Recovery

2 Select Microsoft Excel

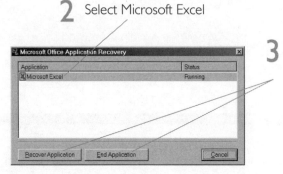

3 Click Recover Application to have Office try to recover the file(s) you were working on, or End Application to close the module with data loss

Re step 5 – files with [Recovered] against them are usually more recent than those with [Original] in the title.

(An alternative approach – you may find it useful to view all file versions and save the best.)

4 In the next dialog, select Send Error Report to email error details to Microsoft, or Don't Send

This is the Document Recovery Task Pane – when you've finished with it, click Close:

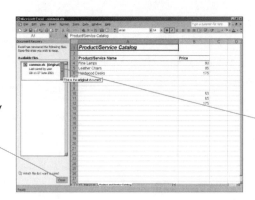

5 Click the bar for the file you want to keep (usually the most recent). In the menu, select Open or View to view it or Save As to save it

Install on Demand

You can use Fast Searching to make it easier to find workbooks through Search.

Click Search Options. In the Indexing Service Settings window, click Advanced. In the next dialog click Modify and select which folders you want indexed. Click OK. Click Update Now to begin the indexing process.

(The above applies to Windows 98, Me and NT 4 users. Users of Windows 2000 should launch Help on how to use Fast Searching. Choose Start, Search, For Files and Folders. Click Search Options in the Search pane, then Indexing Service followed by Help.)

See chapter 13 for how to carry out standard data searches.

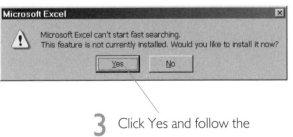

This is just an example: Fast Searching may already have been installed on your PC.

Excel 2002 makes use of a feature which allows users to install programs and program components on demand, only when they're needed. Menu entries, shortcuts and icons relating to the uninstalled features display within the host programs.

An example of Install on Demand is Fast Searching. To install Fast Searching, do the following:

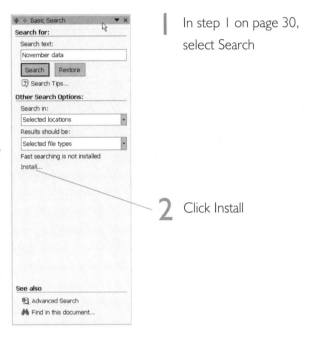

1 In step 1 on page 30, select Search

2 Click Install

3 Click Yes and follow the on-screen instructions

Excel's Task Pane

The use of the Task Pane is also covered at appropriate locations throughout this book.

Excel provides a special pane on the right of the screen which you can use to launch various tasks. There are four incarnations of the Task Pane:

- New Workbook

- Clipboard

- Search

- Insert Clip Art

Using the Task Pane

To display or hide the Task Pane, see the DON'T FORGET tip on page 11. (You can also use a menu route: pull down the View menu and click Task Pane.)

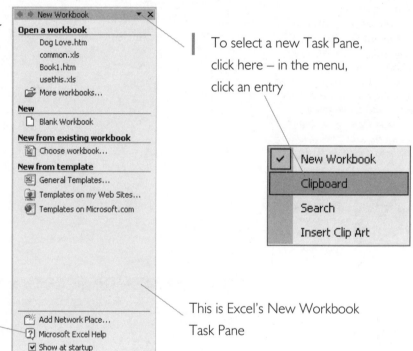

To select a new Task Pane, click here – in the menu, click an entry

This is Excel's New Workbook Task Pane

In the New Workbook Task Pane, click here: to launch

HELP.

Collect and Paste

You can copy multiple items to the Office Clipboard from within any Windows program which supports copy-and-paste, but you can only paste in the last one (except in Excel and other Office modules).

Using Excel 2002, if you want to copy-and-paste multiple items of data and/or pictures into a worksheet, you can now copy as many as 24 items. These are stored in a special version of the Windows Clipboard called the Office Clipboard, which in turn is located in the Task Pane. The Office Clipboard displays a visual representation of the data.

Using the Office Clipboard

From within Excel, use standard procedures to copy multiple examples of data and/or pictures – after the first copy, the Clipboard appears in the Task Pane. Do the following:

To clear the contents of the Office XP Clipboard, click Clear All.

1 Click the data you want to insert – it appears in the active cell

To call up the Office Clipboard at any time, pull down the Edit menu and click Office Clipboard.

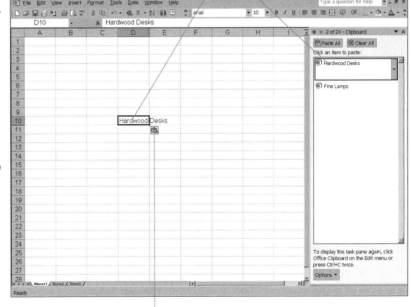

Copying items bigger than 4 Mb (with up to 64 Mb of RAM) or 8 Mb (with more than 64 Mb) to the Office Clipboard will mean it can accept no further data.

For more details of how to carry out copy/move operations, see chapter 3.

2 A Smart Tag appears –
see page 32

Using Smart Tags

Excel 2002 recognises certain types of data and inserts a small purple triangle or blue box in the relevant cell. When you move the mouse pointer over the triangle/box an 'action button' appears which provides access to commands which would otherwise have to be accessed from menus/toolbars or other programs.

Two examples are:

The Paste Options button

Here, we're pasting in '125' as a new value

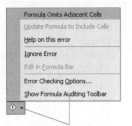

The Trace Error Smart Tag in action

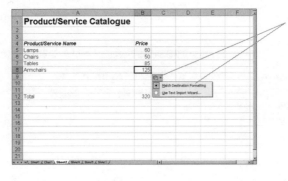

2 Clicking the arrow launches a menu – make a choice

Inserting stock symbols

You can type MSFT and press Enter to insert US stock symbols and have Excel provide Web-based information

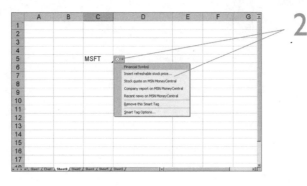

2 Clicking the arrow launches a menu – make a choice

Digital signatures

If you can't find SELFCERT.EXE, go to Control Panel. Double-click Add/ Remove Programs. Select the relevant Office entry and click Add/Remove. Select Add or Remove Features then Next. In the Setup dialog, double-click Office Shared Features. Click the box to the left of Digital Signatures... In the menu, select Run from My Computer. Click Update.

You can attach digital signatures to Excel worksheets, as a way of enhancing security. The signature confirms that the document was sent by you and hasn't been altered in any way, and uses a digital certificate.

Creating digital certificates

1 Locate a file called SELFCERT.EXE (usually in the C:\Program Files\Microsoft Office\Office10\ folder)

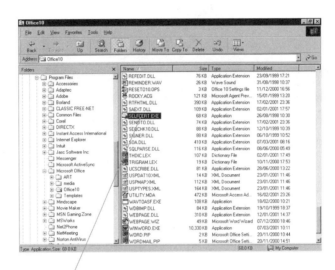

You can also obtain digital certificates from commercial companies. For more information, visit:

http://officeupdate. microsoft.com/office/ redirect/10/Helplinks.asp

and follow the on-screen instructions.

2 Double-click SELFCERT.EXE

Running the procedure here creates a self-certification. Self-certification doesn't carry the weight of certification by a formal certification authority (see the above tip).

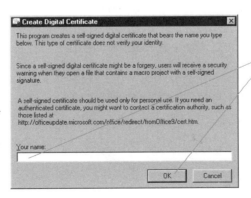

3 Enter your name and confirm

Applying digital signatures

If you're using Excel as a member of an organisation, it may have its own certification authority. Contact your network administrator or IT department for more information.

1 Pull down the Tools menu and click Options.

2 Click the Security tab

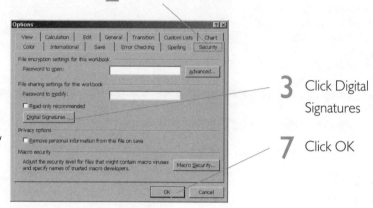

3 Click Digital Signatures

7 Click OK

Digitally signing documents may have no legal validity.

To remove a digital signature, select it here and click Remove.

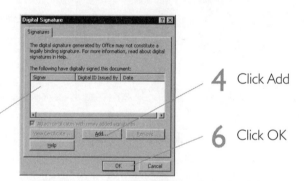

4 Click Add

6 Click OK

You can only apply signatures to files which have been saved (Excel reminds you if this isn't the case). By the same token, saving a file after you've signed it removes the signature.

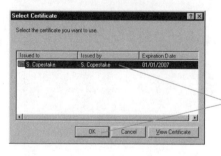

5 Select a certificate and confirm

Worksheet basics

In this chapter, you'll learn how to 'forward-plan' worksheets, to ensure your data is easy to follow. We'll also examine the different types of data you can enter, and look at how to modify it when you've entered it. Excel 2002 has several features which act as shortcuts to data entry; you'll use these to save time and effort. Then you'll discover how to work with number formats; specify suitable data types; insert formulas into cells (including the use of the Range Finder); use the Formula Evaluator to 'parse' formulas; and carry out simple What-If tests.

Finally, you'll resize rows and columns, and insert new cells, rows and columns.

Covers

Chapter Two

Layout planning

As you enter data into your worksheet, use the techniques discussed here (and on page 47) to ensure your data is clear and easily comprehensible.

You should also ensure your worksheet has an effective overall 'look' – see Chapter 13 for more information on how to format worksheets.

When you start Excel 2002, a blank worksheet is automatically created and loaded. This means you can click any cell and start entering data immediately. However, it's a good idea to give some thought to an overall layout strategy before you do this.

Look at the simple worksheet excerpt below:

2		Widgets ordered =	425
3		Price per unit =	0.73
4		Amount due (excluding VAT) =	

Here, the text occupies far more space than the numbers and formulas. The problem has been solved by widening the column containing the text (see page 47 for how to do this). The problem is that this method prevents subsequent lines in the column from being subdivided into further columns.

Look at the next illustration:

2		Widgets ordered =		425
3		Price per unit =		0.73
4		Amount due (excluding VAT) =		

This text has bled into the next column

The second method is often the most flexible.

Here, on the other hand, the final text entry has been allowed to straddle as many adjacent columns as necessary. The proviso here is that you must ensure you leave as many empty adjacent cells as are necessary fully to display the text.

Data types

To force a sequence of digits to be input as text, precede them by a single quotation mark. For instance, to type in 1234 as text type:

'1234

In Chapter 1, we looked at how to key in simple data. Now, we'll examine the types of data you can enter in more detail.

Excel 2002 determines the type of data entered into a cell by the sequence of characters keyed. The types are:

- numbers (i.e. digits, decimal point, #, %, +, −)

- text (any other string of characters)

- formulas (always preceded by =)

The worksheet excerpt below shows these data types in action:

These are default alignments. To apply a new alignment, select the cell(s). Right-click over them. In the menu, click Format Cells. In the Format Cells dialog, click the Alignment tab. Select a new alignment. Click OK.

B2 contains text (aligned to the left of the cell)

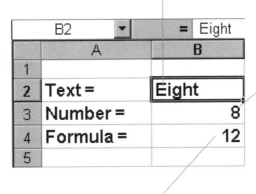

B3 contains the number 8 (aligned to the right of the cell)

B4 contains the hidden formula: =8+4

If you want to display the underlying formula rather than the result, select the relevant cell and press:

Ctrl+'

(The ' character is at the top left of the keyboard, below the function keys.)

When a formula has been inserted into a cell, Excel 2002 evaluates it. The resultant value – in the case of B4 above, 12 – is shown, aligned to the right.

For more information on formulas, see pages 43–45.

Modifying existing data

Re the tip below – the Undo and Redo buttons may not be in the main body of the toolbar. If so, click this button:

and access them in the fly-out.

You can amend the contents of a cell in two ways:

• via the Formula bar

• from within the cell

When you use either of these methods, Excel 2002 enters a special state known as Edit Mode.

Amending existing data using the Formula bar

Click the cell whose contents you want to change. Then click in the Formula bar. Make the appropriate revisions and/or additions. Then press Enter. Excel updates the relevant cell.

Amending existing data internally

Click the cell whose contents you want to change. Press F2. Make the appropriate revisions and/or additions *within the cell*. Then press Enter.

The illustration below shows a section from a blank workbook:

To redo an action, click the following button in the Standard toolbar:

In the list, select a redo action (but note that selecting an early operation – one near the bottom – will include all later operations).

To redo an action, click the following button in the Standard toolbar:

In the list, select a redo action (but note that selecting an early operation – one near the bottom – will include all later operations).

A magnified view of cell G15, in Edit Mode (note the flashing insertion point)

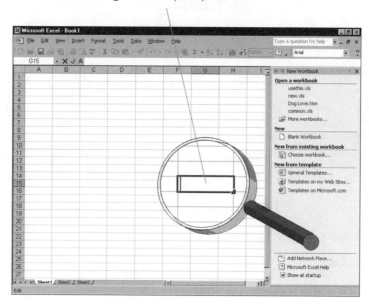

AutoComplete

If in-cell editing (see page 38) doesn't work, pull down the Tools menu and click Options. Select the Edit tab, then tick Edit directly in cell. Finally, click OK.

Excel 2002 has a range of features which save you time and effort:

- AutoComplete

- AutoFill

- AutoCorrect

AutoComplete examines the contents of the active column and tries to anticipate what you're about to type. Look at the next illustration:

You can also use another technique. Instead of starting to type in the repeat entry, right-click over the cell. In the menu, click Pick From List. Now do the following:

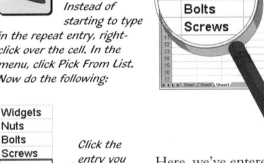

Click the entry you want to use

Here, we've entered a series of text values into cells B4:B7. If you want to duplicate any of these entries in B8, you can (in this instance) simply type in the first letter then press Enter.

Use the example here as a guide – you may have to enter more than one letter...

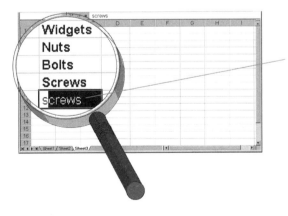

Typing in 's' has prompted Excel 2002 to insert the correct term...

AutoFill

AutoFill extends formatting and formulas in lists.

Types of series you can use AutoFill to complete include:

- *1st Period, 2nd Period, 3rd Period etc.*
- *Mon, Tue, Wed etc.*
- *Quarter 1, Quarter 2, Quarter 3 etc.*
- *Week1, Week2, Week3 etc.*

Data series don't need to contain every possibility. For instance, you could have:

- *1st Period, 3rd Period, 5th Period etc.*
- *Mon, Thu, Sun, Wed etc.*
- *Quarter 1, Quarter 4, Quarter 3, Quarter 2 etc.*
- *Week2, Week6, Week10, Week14 etc.*

Excel 2002 lets you insert data series automatically. This is a very useful and timesaving feature. Look at the illustration below:

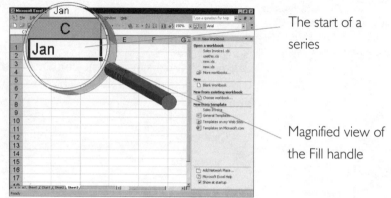

The start of a series

Magnified view of the Fill handle

If you wanted to insert month names in successive cells in column C, you could do so manually. But there's a much easier way. You can use Excel's AutoFill feature.

Using AutoFill to create a series

Type in the first element(s) of the series in consecutive cells. Select all the cells. Then position the mouse pointer over the Fill handle in the bottom right-hand corner of the last cell (the pointer changes to a crosshair). Drag the handle over the cells into which you want to extend the series (in the example above, over C2:C12). When you release the mouse button, Excel 2002 extrapolates the initial entry or entries into the appropriate series:

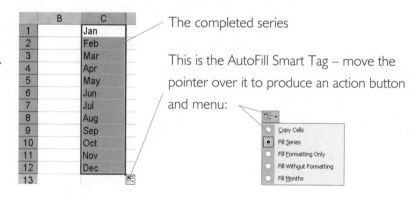

The completed series

This is the AutoFill Smart Tag – move the pointer over it to produce an action button and menu:

Number formats

You can customise the way cell contents (e.g. numbers and dates/times) display in Excel 2002. You can specify:

- at what point numbers are rounded up

- how minus values are displayed (for example, whether they display in red, and/or with '–' in front of them)

- (in the case of currency values) which currency symbol (e.g. £ or $) is used

- (in the case of dates and times) the generic display type (e.g. *day/month/year* or *month/year*)

Available formats are organised under general categories. These include: Number, Currency and Fraction.

Specifying a number format

Select the cells whose contents you want to customise. Pull down the Format menu and click Cells. Now do the following:

Ensure the Number tab is active

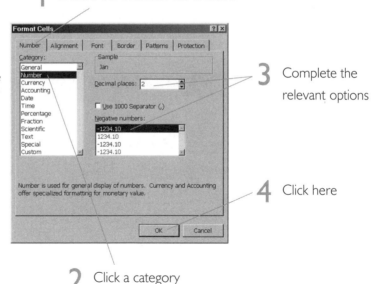

3 Complete the relevant options

4 Click here

2 Click a category

Data validation

To apply a character limit, select Text Length in step 3. Follow step 4. In step 5, enter min. and max. limits (e.g. '4' and '8'). Carry out step 6.

You can have Excel 2002 'validate' data. This can mean:

- restricting cells so only data which is within specific number or time limits can be entered

- restricting cells so only a specific number of characters can be entered

Applying data validation

Select one or more cells. Pull down the Data menu and do the following:

Re step 5 – depending on the type of limit imposed in step 3, you can enter:

- *values*
- *formulas*
- *cell addresses*

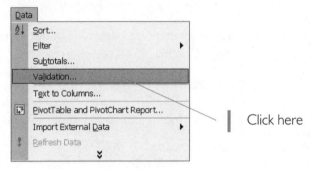

Click here

Select the Input Message and Error Alert tabs to set data entry and error messages.

2 Ensure the Settings tab is active

Re step 4 – note that you can select from these operators:

- *between*
- *not between*
- *equal to*
- *not equal to*
- *greater than*
- *less than*
- *greater than or equal to*
- *less than or equal to*

(The dialog changes according to which is chosen.)

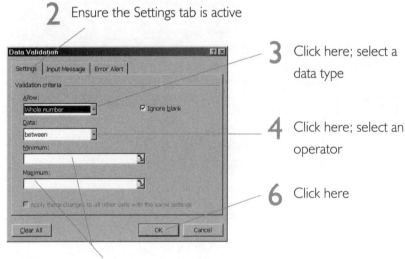

3 Click here; select a data type

4 Click here; select an operator

6 Click here

5 Specify 1 or 2 limits (as appropriate)

Formulas – an overview

Formulas are cell entries which define how other values relate to each other.

As a very simple example, consider the following:

The underlying formula – see below

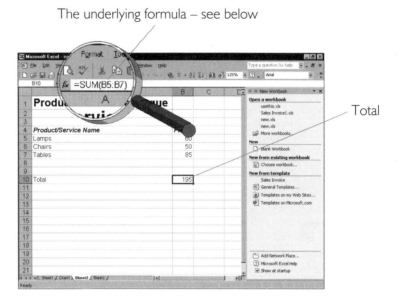

Total

Here, a cell has been defined which returns the total of cells B5:B7. Obviously, in this instance you could insert the total easily enough yourself because the individual values are so small, and because we're only dealing with a small number of cells. But what happens if the cell values are larger and/or more numerous, or – more to the point – if they're liable to change frequently?

The answer is to insert a formula which carries out the necessary calculation automatically.

If you look at the Formula bar in the illustration, you'll see the formula which does this:

=SUM(B5:B7)

Many Excel formulas are much more complex than this, but the principles remain the same.

Inserting a formula

All formulas in Excel 2002 begin with an equals sign. This is usually followed by a permutation of the following:

- an operand (cell reference, e.g. B4)

- a function (e.g. the summation function, SUM)

- an arithmetical operator (+, –, / and *)

- comparison operators (<, >, <=, >= and =)

Excel supports a very wide range of functions organised into numerous categories. For more information on how to insert functions, see chapter 6.

The mathematical operators are (in the order in which they appear in the list): *plus, minus, divide* and *multiply*.

The comparison operators are (in the order in which they appear in the list): *less than, greater than, less than or equal to, greater than or equal to* and *equals*.

There are two ways to enter formulas:

Entering a formula directly into the cell

Click the cell in which you want to insert a formula. Then type = followed by your formula. When you've finished, press Enter.

Entering a formula into the Formula bar

This is usually the most convenient method.

Click the cell in which you want to insert a formula. Then click in the Formula bar. Type = followed by your formula. When you've finished, press Enter or do the following:

Click here

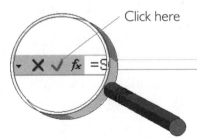

The Formula Evaluator

When formulas become complex (as they frequently do), it can be difficult to see how Excel arrives at the eventual result. However, you can now use a feature called Formula Evaluator to step through each calculation.

You can use a feature called Range Finder to visually redefine the cells a formula applies to.
When you're creating or editing a formula and Excel surrounds the arguments with a blue or green border, drag one or more of these to a new cell selection. The formula is updated automatically.

Using the Formula Evaluator

1 Select the cell which contains the formula. Pull down the Tools menu and click Formula Auditing, Evaluate Formula

See page 80 for how to launch the Formula Evaluator on-the-fly, via a Smart Tag.

2 Click Evaluate – repeat as often as required

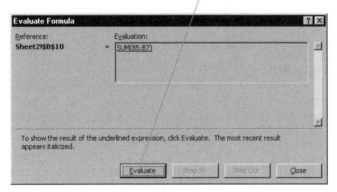

3 Each step is shown here – click Close when you've finished

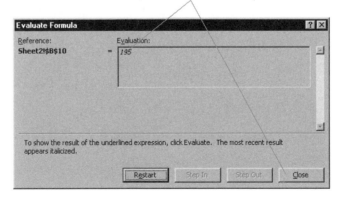

Simple What-If tests

The power of a worksheet is only really appreciated when you carry out 'What-If' tests. These involve adjusting the numbers in selected cells in order to observe the effect on formulas throughout the worksheet. Any such changes 'ripple through' the worksheet.

In the simple example below, C4 has the following formula:

$=C2*C3$

which multiplies the contents of C2 by C3.

	A	B	C
1			
2		Widgets ordered =	425
3		Price per unit =	0.73
4		Amount due (excluding VAT) =	310.25

If changes you make to data don't produce the relevant update, pull down the Tools menu and click Options. In the Options dialog, select the Calculation tab. Click Automatic in the Calculation section, followed by OK.

By entering alternative values into C2 or C3, you can watch the changes filter through to C4. In the next illustration, the value in C2 has changed; Excel 2002 has automatically calculated the effect on the total:

	A	B	C
1			
2		Widgets ordered =	562
3		Price per unit =	0.73
4		Amount due (excluding VAT) =	410.26

The change in C2 has automatically adjusted the C4 total

Amending row/column sizes

Sooner or later, you'll find it necessary to resize rows or columns. This necessity arises when there is too much data in cells to display adequately. You can enlarge or shrink single or multiple rows/columns.

Changing row height

To change one row's height, click the row heading. If you want to change multiple rows, hold down Ctrl and click the appropriate extra headings. Then place the mouse pointer (it changes to a cross) just under the row heading(s). Hold down the left mouse button and drag up or down to decrease or increase the row(s) respectively. Release the mouse button to confirm the operation.

Excel has a useful 'Best Fit' feature. When the mouse pointer has changed to:

(or the reverse, with the arrowed line horizontal in the case of columns), double-click to have the row(s) or column(s) adjust themselves automatically to their contents.

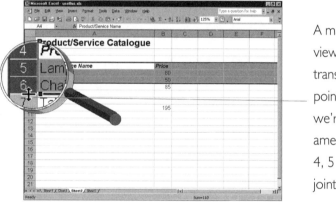

A magnified view of the transformed pointer – here, we're amending rows 4, 5 and 6 jointly

Changing column width

To change one column's width, click the column heading. If you want to change multiple columns, hold down Ctrl and click the appropriate extra headings. Then place the mouse pointer (it changes to a cross) just to the right of the column heading(s). Hold down the left mouse button and drag right or left to widen or narrow the column(s) respectively.

Release the mouse button to confirm the operation.

Inserting cells, rows or columns

You can insert additional cells, rows or columns into worksheets.

If you select cells in more than one row or column, Excel 2002 inserts the equivalent number of new rows or columns.

Inserting a new row or column

First, select one or more cells within the row(s) or column(s) where you want to carry out the insert operation. Now pull down the Insert menu and click Rows or Columns, as appropriate. Excel 2002 inserts the new row(s) or column(s) immediately.

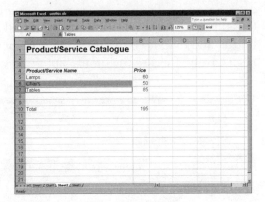

Here, one new column or two new rows are being added

Inserting a new cell range

Select the range where you want to insert the new cells. Pull down the Insert menu and click Cells. Now carry out step 1 or step 2 below. Finally, follow step 3.

1 Click here to have Excel make room for the new cells by moving the selected range *to the right*

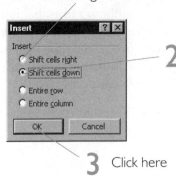

2 Click here to have Excel make room for the new cells by moving the selected range *down*

3 Click here

Copy/move techniques

In this chapter, you'll learn how to copy and move cells, techniques which will greatly enhance your use of Excel. You'll copy/move data within the host worksheet, to another worksheet and to another (open) workbook. You'll also perform copy operations which are restricted to specific cell aspects, then make use of a shortcut which makes copying data to adjacent cells even easier. You'll also move worksheets to a different location within the host workbook (and to another workbook).

Finally, you'll drag-and-drop data directly into Excel 2002 from within Internet Explorer.

Covers

Chapter Three

Copying and moving cells

You can also use a variant of AutoFill to copy data. Select a cell range then move the mouse pointer over the Fill handle (for more on this, see page 40). Hold down Ctrl and drag the handle over as many adjacent cells as you want to copy the data into.

(Note: if you carry out this procedure in respect of more than 1 cell but don't hold down Ctrl, or if you carry it out in respect of a single cell but do hold down Ctrl, Excel extrapolates – rather than copies – the data.)

When you copy or move data in cells which contain formulas, Excel adjusts the cell references.

When you perform a copy operation, the mouse pointer looks like this:

In a move operation, on the other hand, it looks like this:

Excel 2002 lets you copy or move cells:

- within the same worksheet

- from one worksheet to another

- from one worksheet to another worksheet in a different workbook

Copying data within the same worksheet

Select the cell range which contains the data you want to copy. Move the mouse pointer over the range border; it changes to an arrow. Hold down one Ctrl key; left-click and drag the range to the new location. Release the mouse button.

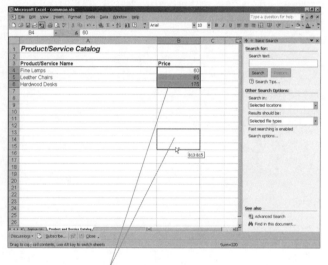

Cells in the course of being copied

Moving data within the same worksheet

Select the cell range which contains the data you want to move. Place the mouse pointer over the range border; it changes to an arrow. Left-click and drag the range to the new location. Release the mouse button.

Advanced copying

Re step 1 – if you haven't used it much (or if you've expanded the Formatting toolbar), the Copy button may be on the Standard toolbar fly-out instead. If it is, click:

to access it.

Excel 2002 allows you to be highly specific about which cell components are copied. You can use a special technique to limit the copy operation to any of the following (but only one at a time):

- the cell format

- underlying formulas

- cell values

- any data validation rules you've set

- all cell contents and formats

Performing specific copy operations

Select the data you want to copy. Then refer to the Standard toolbar and do the following:

Click the Copy button

After step 2, pull down the Edit menu and click Paste Special. In the Paste Special dialog, select a data component (e.g. Formulas or Validation). You can also select an operation (e.g. Multiply or Divide) to apply this to the copied data.

Optional – click Transpose to change columns of copied data to rows (or vice versa). Finally, click OK.

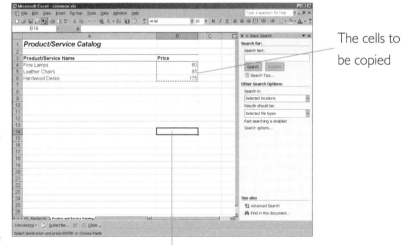

The cells to be copied

2 Click the upper left cell in the Paste Area (the cell range into which you want the data copied)

External copy/move operations

You can easily copy or move a range of cells between worksheets and workbooks.

Moving data to another Worksheet

When you move the mouse pointer over the appropriate tab, Excel 2002 highlights it: Drag the cell range back into the worksheet area (the second worksheet is now displayed) and position it in the correct location.

Select the cell range which contains the data you want to move. Place the mouse pointer over the range border; it changes to an arrow. Hold down the Alt key; left-click and drag the range onto the relevant worksheet tab:

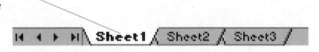

The Worksheet tab area at the base of the screen

Position the range using the techniques discussed in the DON'T FORGET tip.

Copying data to another Worksheet

Select the cell range which contains the data you want to copy. Place the mouse pointer over the range border; it changes to an arrow. Hold down the Alt key and one Ctrl key; left-click and drag the range onto the relevant worksheet tab, then position it using the techniques discussed in the DON'T FORGET tip.

Moving data to another Workbook

First open both workbooks in separate windows (for how to do this, see your Windows documentation). Select the cell range which contains the data you want to move. Place the mouse pointer over the range border; it changes to an arrow. Left-click and drag the range onto the relevant worksheet in the second workbook.

Before you move/copy data to another workbook, pre-select the appropriate worksheet.

Copying data to another Workbook

First open both workbooks in separate windows. Select the cell range containing the data to be copied. Place the mouse pointer over the border; it changes to an arrow. Hold down one Ctrl key; left-click and drag the range onto the relevant worksheet in the second workbook.

Moving worksheets

You can perform two kinds of move operation on worksheets. You can:

- rearrange the worksheet order within a given workbook

- transfer a worksheet to another workbook

Rearranging worksheets

To select a single worksheet, click the relevant sheet tab in the Worksheet tab area. (Or select more than one worksheet by holding down Ctrl as you click multiple tabs.) With the mouse pointer still over the selected tab(s), hold down the left mouse button and drag them to their new location in the tab area. Release the mouse button to confirm the operation.

Moving worksheets to another workbook

To select a single worksheet, click the relevant sheet tab in the worksheet tab area. (Or select more than one worksheet by holding down Ctrl as you click multiple tabs.) Pull down the Edit menu and click Move or Copy Sheet. Now do the following:

Click here; select the new host workbook from the drop-down list

2 Click the worksheet in front of which you want the transferred sheet(s) to appear

3 Click here

Copying data from Internet Explorer

To use method A, select the relevant data in Internet Explorer. Press Ctrl+C to copy it, or Ctrl+X to move it. Position the cursor at the location in Excel 2002 where you want the data inserted. Press Shift+Insert.

A special relationship exists between Excel 2002 and Internet Explorer 5.x or later. Because the Windows Clipboard now recognises the HTML file format, you can:

A. copy data from Internet Explorer and paste it into Excel

B. drag-and-drop data from Internet Explorer into Excel

Using method B.

With Excel 2002 and Internet Explorer both open in separate windows, do the following:

Select the relevant data in Internet Explorer, then drag it into Excel 2002

Re step 1 and the above tip – use the mouse to select data in Internet Explorer.

To select all data within Internet Explorer, press Ctrl+A.

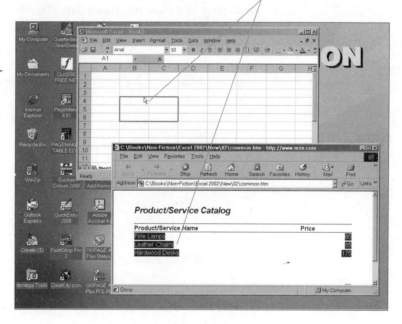

2 Release the mouse button – Excel inserts the data

Workbook management

In this chapter, you'll learn how to create new workbooks, then save and reopen them. You'll also save workbooks as templates and as HTML files (for use on the Internet and intranets), interactively (so users can work with the data) and non-interactively. You'll also learn how to republish HTML files automatically when you save changes to the originating workbook. Then you'll have Excel 2002 save your work automatically, at an interval you set. Finally, you'll save (and reopen) your overall environment as a workspace, and then close all active workbooks.

Covers

Chapter Four

Creating new workbooks

Creating new workbooks is made easy by the provision of templates. A template is a pre-designed workbook which is ready to use. The templates supplied with Excel 2002 contain:

- numerous pre-defined fields

- several pre-defined worksheets

- pre-defined formatting

- special buttons which you can click to launch features directly

As well as using the templates provided, you can design your own – see page 59. Alternatively you can create a new blank workbook – see the HOT TIP.

Creating a workbook

Refer to the Task Pane and do the following:

Re step 1 – to create a new blank workbook, click Blank Workbook.

You can open Web templates. In step 3, click Templates on Microsoft.com instead. Now follow the on-screen instructions.

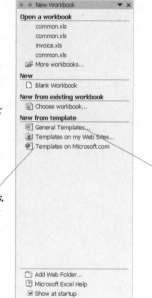

Click General Templates

...cont'd

User-generated templates are stored in the General tab – see page 59.

2 Click Spreadsheet Solutions

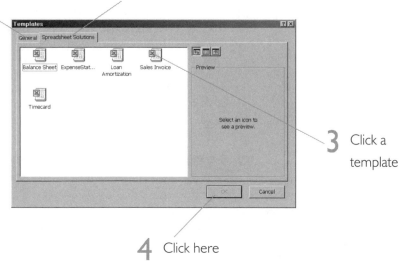

3 Click a template

4 Click here

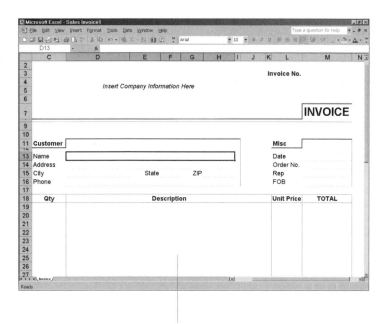

A worksheet in a new workbook based on the Sales Invoice template

Saving workbooks

It's important to save your work at frequent intervals, in order to avoid data loss in the event of a hardware fault or power interruption.

Saving a workbook for the first time

Pull down the File menu and click Save. Or press Ctrl+S. Now do the following:

2 Click here. In the drop-down list, click a drive/ folder combination

*Re step 2 –
click any
buttons here:
for access to
the relevant
folders.
(For instance, to save files
to your Desktop, click
Desktop.)*

*Note that you
can use a
shortcut for
either save
method.
Click this icon:*

in the Standard toolbar.

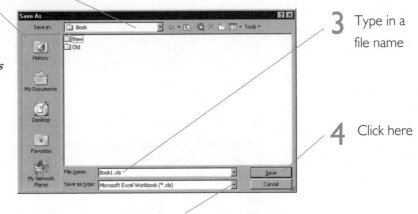

3 Type in a file name

4 Click here

Click here. In the list, click the format you want to save to

Saving previously saved workbooks

Pull down the File menu and click Save. Or press Ctrl+S. No dialog launches; instead, Excel saves the latest version of your workbook to disk, overwriting the previous version.

Saving workbooks as templates

Workbooks you've created and formatted can be saved as templates, for future use. When you've done this, you can base new documents on them (see pages 56-57), which represents a considerable saving in time and effort.

By default, workbook templates are saved to the following folder:

\WINDOWS\Application Data\Microsoft\Templates

and appear as icons in the Templates dialog's General tab (page 57).

Saving a workbook as a template

Open the relevant workbook. Pull down the File menu and click Save As. Carry out the following steps:

If you want to save your template to a nonstandard folder, follow step 1. Click the arrow to the right of the Save in: field. In the list, select a drive. Now double-click the necessary folder(s) here:

Finally, perform steps 2–3.

2 Name the template

3 Click here

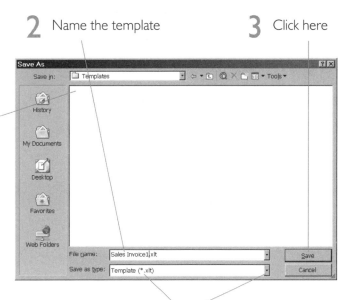

Make sure Template (*.xlt) is shown. If it isn't, click the arrow and select it from the drop-down list

Saving to the Internet

To create a shortcut to a Web/FTP folder, you must have:

• *a live Internet connection*

• *rights to view/save files*

• *its URL*

To create a shortcut to an intranet folder, you must have the following:

• *a network connection*

• *rights to view/save files*

• *its network address*

You can save documents (usually in HTML – HyperText Markup Language – format) to network, Web or FTP servers. You can do this so long as you've created a shortcut to the folder that contains them.

Creating shortcuts to Web/FTP folders

1 Open the Excel Open or Save As dialog and do the following:

3 Double-click Add Network Place

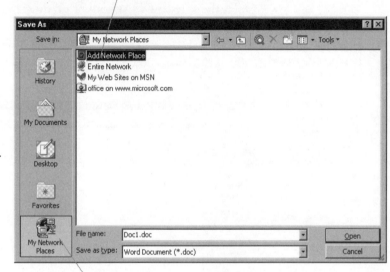

Re step 2 – users of Windows NT 4 or 98 should click Web Folders instead. In step 3, double-click Add Web Folder and follow the on-screen instructions.

Users of Windows NT 4 or 98 – to create a Web folder, get details of servers which support Web folders from your:

• *system administrator*

or

• *Internet Service Provider*

2 In Windows 2000 or Me, click here

4 Complete the Add Network Place wizard

Creating shortcuts to local network folders
This requires a different procedure.

Windows 2000/Me users should use My Network Places, while Windows NT 4.0 and 98 users should use Network Neighborhood. (For how to do this, see your system administrator.)

Interactive v. non-interactive saving

You can save data to Web pages (on the Internet or intranets) in two ways:

- non-interactively

- interactively

Both methods have one overriding advantage: it isn't necessary to have access to Excel 2002 in order to view the end result.

Non-interactive saving

This is the method to use if you only want users to view, not interact with, your data. Users need only have:

1. access to the Internet or an intranet

2. any appropriate browser (e.g. Internet Explorer)

Interactive saving

Interactively means that users viewing your data can also work with it in (basically) the same way that you do in Excel 2002. For instance, they can:

- rearrange cell ranges

- enter/update values

- calculate data

- implement sorts and filters

As with non-interactive saving, users can view interactive data in their browser, without needing to have installed Excel 2002. There are, however, additional, more stringent requirements. Users must have:

1. Internet Explorer 4.01 or later

2. access to the Office Web Components

When you publish interactively, retain a master copy of the originating workbook. You can then amend this as required and republish it to the Web.

Note that items you can publish with interactivity include:

- *cell ranges*
- *worksheets*
- *print areas*
- *charts*

However, you may lose some formatting or features in the case of charts.

Preparing to save to the Web

There are several steps you should take before you begin any of the procedures on pages 63–65:

To publish your Excel files on the Web, you must have a live Internet connection.

To work with interactively saved data, you must have the following:

- *Internet Explorer 4.1 or later*
- *an appropriate Microsoft Office license*

Re step 6 – if you're publishing your data in .XLS format, carry out a different procedure: select Print Preview in Excel 2002's File menu to preview it.
Press Esc when you've finished.

1 Make sure your original Excel 2002 data is complete and correct (inc. the formatting)

2 Save the definitive version of your Excel workbook as a .XLS file, in the normal way, and keep this secure

3 Decide whether disseminating your data in .XLS format will be sufficient. This is an option if you happen to know that everyone who will view it has access to Excel 2002. If this is the case, jump to page 63 or 64, as appropriate. If it isn't, first carry out the remaining steps below

4 Decide whether you want to save to interactive or non-interactive Web pages (see page 61)

5 It's a good idea – before you make your data available publicly – to save a test version of your Web page on your own PC. This means you can open it in your browser and confirm that everything is as it should be. If it isn't, you can re-export your data after you've made the necessary corrections within the original Excel 2002 file (see step 2)

6 Preview the Web page (see page 63 for non-interactive previewing and step 10 on page 65 for interactive previewing)

7 Decide where you want to put the Web page

Non-interactive saving

Previewing your work before saving

Pull down the File menu and do the following:

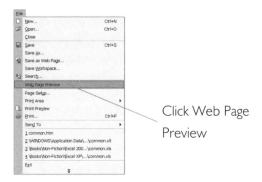

Click Web Page Preview

Before you can save files to Web folders or FTP sites, you must first have carried out the relevant procedures. See page 60.

Your browser now launches, with your work displayed in it. To close it when you've finished using it, press Alt+F4.

Publishing workbooks non-interactively

Pull down the File menu and click Save as Web Page. Then do the following:

Re step 1 – carry out one of the following procedures according to which version of Windows you're running:

- *Windows NT 4 and 98 users – use Network Neighborhood to save to a local network folder and Web Folders to save to a Web or FTP folder*
- *Windows 2000 and Me users – use My Network Places to save to a local network folder or to a Web or FTP folder*

1 | Click here. In the drop-down list, select a recipient – see the HOT TIP

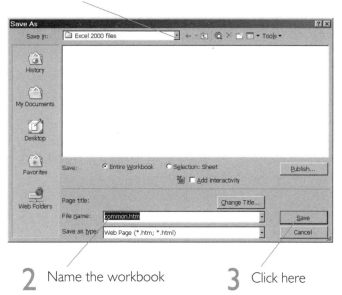

2 Name the workbook

3 Click here

Interactive saving

You can also use the procedures described here to save workbook components e.g.:

• single worksheets

• a chart

• a cell range

non-interactively. Follow steps 1–11, as appropriate, but in step 5 ensure that Add interactivity... is *not* ticked.

You can combine interactive and non-interactive material in a single Web page. (You can also use data from separate Office programs.)

This is a useful technique since it allows you to combine items which logically belong together. For example, you could create a page containing non-interactive data, an interactive chart, your logo and related text items...

Interactive saving sometimes results in not all formatting or features being retained.

On page 63, we looked at how to save data non-interactively. This method produces HTML files which can be viewed in more or less any browser, without the need to have access to Excel 2002. If all you want is to have your data viewed, then this is what you need.

However, you can also publish Excel 2002 worksheets *interactively* to the Internet or intranets. This technique allows users to interact with your data.

Publishing interactive worksheets

1 Pull down the File menu and click Save as Web Page

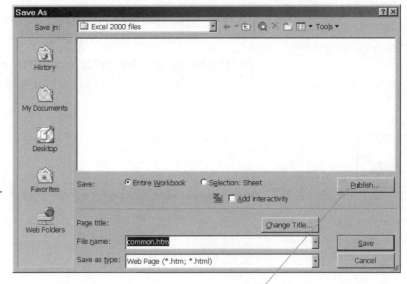

2 Click Publish

...cont'd

In the Viewing options section, make the appropriate selection in line with the following:

- *select Spreadsheet Functionality if you're exporting a spreadsheet or filtered list*
- *select PivotTable functionality if you're exporting a PivotTable*
- *select Chart functionality if you're exporting a chart (but note that you must publish the chart separately from other worksheet contents)*

3 Click here; in the list, select the type of data you want to publish

4 Optional – specify a data item

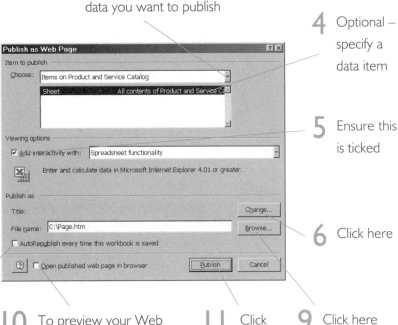

5 Ensure this is ticked

6 Click here

Tick AutoRepublish every time this workbook is saved to have Excel automatically update your Web file each time you carry out a save operation. (Make sure you select the Refresh option in your browser – e.g. press F5 in I.E. 5.x – when viewing.)

10 To preview your Web page in your browser, select Open published web page in browser

11 Click here

9 Click here and complete the Browse dialog

7 Name the published data

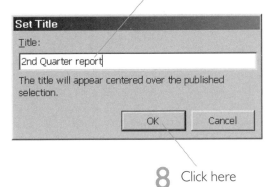

8 Click here

Using AutoSave

By default, Excel saves your work every 10 minutes. This is a very useful feature which helps to ensure that you don't lose data in the event of a crash or power failure. However, you should not use AutoSave as a substitute for saving your work in the normal way – regard it instead as a useful supplement in your data backup schedule.

Customising AutoSave

Pull down the Tools menu and click Options. Do the following:

You can turn AutoSave off (though it's hard to imagine a good reason for doing to) by unticking this:

1 Select the Save tab

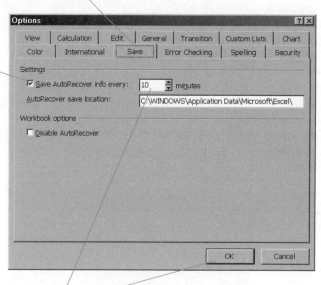

Excel 2002 lets you save your workbooks to a variety of third-party formats. To do this, carry out steps 1-4 on page 58. In step 1, however, select the relevant external format.

To close down the active workbook, pull down the File menu and select Close. (To close all open workbooks, hold down one Shift key as you pull down the menu and click Close All.)
Excel warns you if there is any unsaved data – click Yes to proceed.

2 Type in a new save interval (in minutes) then click OK

Opening workbooks

We saw earlier that you can create new workbooks in Excel. You can also open Excel 2002 workbooks you've already created.

Refer to the Task Pane on the right of the screen and perform steps 1-2 (if you haven't recently opened the workbook you want to open, carry out steps 3-4 instead):

If the Task Pane isn't visible, choose View, Task Pane.

Re step 4 – if you store workbooks in one folder, you can have the Open dialog default to it.

Pull down the Tools menu and click Options. In the Options dialog, activate the General tab. In the Default file location: field, type in the default folder. Finally, click OK.

You can also launch the Open dialog directly from within Excel. Press Ctrl+O.

You can copy, rename or delete workbooks from within the Open dialog.

Right-click any workbook entry in the main part of the dialog. In the menu, click the desired option. Now carry out the appropriate action.

An example: to rename a workbook, click Rename in the menu. Type in the new name and press Enter.

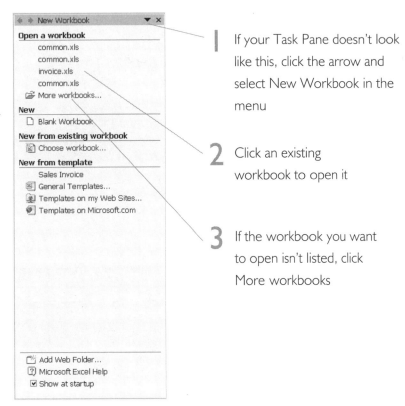

1 If your Task Pane doesn't look like this, click the arrow and select New Workbook in the menu

2 Click an existing workbook to open it

3 If the workbook you want to open isn't listed, click More workbooks

4 Use the Open dialog to find and select the file you want to open. Click Open

Opening Web/intranet workbooks

You can open workbooks stored at FTP sites on the World Wide Web or on intranets.

If the Web toolbar isn't currently on-screen, move the mouse pointer over any existing toolbar and right-click. In the menu which appears, click Web. Now do the following:

To open Internet workbooks, you must have a live connection to the Internet.

Click Go

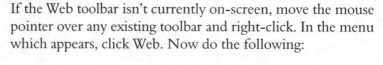

After step 4, the Web/ intranet site selected in step 3 is opened in your browser.

2 Click here

3 Type in the relevant address

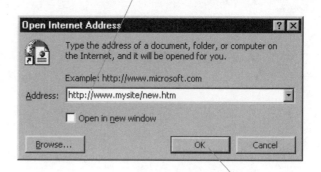

Re step 3 – to open an Excel workbook on an intranet, you might type:

http://server/mine.xls

where 'mine.xls' is the workbook, and 'server' the name of the server.

4 Click here

Reopening HTML files

See pages 60–65 for how to generate HTML files from Excel 2002 workbooks/worksheets.

Because Microsoft regards HTML as having the same status as its own proprietary formats, when you export HTML files in Excel 2002 they can be edited directly from within Internet Explorer 5.x or later with little or no loss of data or formatting. Excel calls this process 'round-tripping'.

The lack of deterioration can be demonstrated further with the help of examples. Study the two illustrations below:

You can edit Excel-produced HTML files directly from within Internet Explorer 5.x or higher. Click this button in the toolbar:

Excel automatically opens the HTML file.

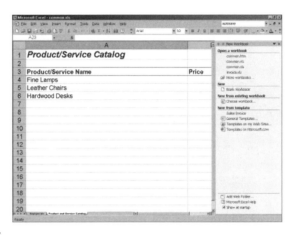

The original workbook...

In Excel 2002, more formatting and features can be brought back into Excel, irrespective of whether interactivity was employed in the original save.

Here, saving the Excel 2002 workbook to HTML and reopening it has produced only two minor changes:

- the original Zoom setting has not been retained
- gridlines are not visible (to rectify this, choose Tools, Options. In the Options dialog, select the General tab and tick Gridlines. Click OK.)

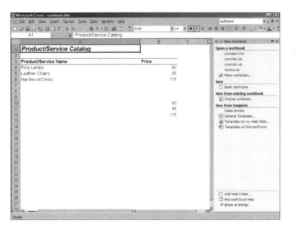

The HTML file after being reopened in Excel 2002

Using workspaces

Sometimes when you work with Excel 2002, you'll require:

- more than one workbook open simultaneously

- multiple worksheets open simultaneously

Instead of having to open each component separately, you can save details of your current working environment as a 'workspace'. When you've done this, you can simply reopen the workspace; Excel 2002 then opens the constituent workbooks/worksheets for you.

Saving the current environment as a workspace

Pull down the File menu and click Save Workspace. Now carry out the following steps:

Re step 3 – the default file name for a workspace is 'resume.xlw'. Change this if you want.

Repeat step 2 as necessary, until you locate the relevant folder.

To reopen a workspace, press Ctrl+O. In the Open dialog, select Workspaces (*.xlw) in the Files of type field. Locate the workspace and click OK.

1 Click here. In the drop-down list, select a drive

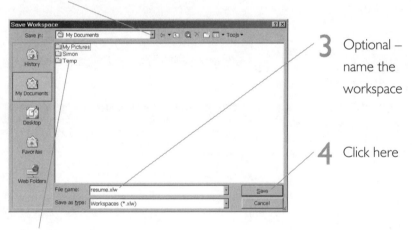

3 Optional – name the workspace

4 Click here

2 Double-click the folder where you want to save the workspace

Cell referencing

In this chapter, you'll learn how to define cell references. You'll apply relative and absolute references, then discover how to use an older but easier-to-use system: R1C1 referencing. Next, you'll apply names to cells (a technique which makes cell manipulation much more convenient) and formulas, and then delete existing names. Finally, you'll have Excel replace references in formulas with their equivalent names, paste names into formulas via the Formula Bar and learn about additional cell operators (you'll also correct errors in them via Smart Tags).

Covers

Chapter Five

Relative references

Excel 2002 lets you define cell references in various ways. Look at the next illustration:

	A	B	C	D	E
1					
2		**Product**	**Unit Price**	**Quantity**	**Amount due**
3		Widgets	£0.07	425	£29.75
4		Nuts	£0.13	246	
5		Bolts	£0.08	380	

You can also use 3D referencing to analyse data in the same cell(s) throughout a number of worksheets. For instance:

=SUM(Sheet6:Sheet10!J45)

would add all values contained in cell J45 on all worksheets between (and including) Sheet 6 and Sheet 10.

3D referencing works with various functions including AVERAGE, COUNT, MAX and MIN.

(For more information, see page 135.)

The following formula has been inserted in cell E3:

C3*D3

This tells Excel to multiply the contents of C3 by D3. C3 and D3 are defined in relation to E3: C3 is in the same row (3) but two columns to the left (C), while D3 is in the same row but *one* column to the left. Excel calls this 'relative referencing'.

That these are relative references can be shown in the following way. If we use the techniques discussed on page 40 (AutoFill) to extend the formula in E3 to E4 and E5, this is the result:

	C	D	E
1			
2	Unit Price	Quantity	Amount due
3	0.07	425	=C3*D3
4	0.13	246	=C4*D4
5	0.08	380	=C5*D5

Extrapolated cell references

The formulas in E3:E5 have been made visible by pressing Ctrl+'. (To type ' press the key directly beneath the Esc key.)

To hide the formulas again, repeat this.

Excel 2002 has extrapolated the references intelligently, correctly divining that the formula in E4 should be C4*D4, and that in E5 C5*D5.

Compare this process with the use of absolute (i.e. unchanging) references on page 73.

Absolute references

We've seen – on page 72 – how useful relative cell references can be. However, there are situations when you need to refer to one or more cells in a way which *doesn't* vary according to circumstances.

You can have 'mixed' references, where the row is absolute and the column relative or vice versa.
If you copy mixed references, the relative reference updates but the absolute doesn't.

Look at the next illustration:

	A	B	C	D	E	F
1	VAT rate=	17.50%				
2		**Product**	**Unit Price**	**Quantity**	**Amount due**	**VAT**
3		Widgets	£0.07	425	£29.75	£5.21
4		Nuts	£0.13	246	£31.98	
5		Bolts	£0.08	380	£30.40	

The reason the VAT rate is entered separately from the calculation is convenience: if the rate changes, it's much easier to update one entry, rather than several.

Cell F3 contains a formula which multiplies E3 by B1. If this were inserted as:

=E3*B1

extrapolating the formula over F4 and F5 (with the technique we used on page 72) would produce:

=E4*B2

and

=E5*B3

respectively.

You can also use mixed cell references – i.e. combinations of relative and absolute references.

Clearly, this is incorrect (in this instance) because the cell in which the VAT rate is entered doesn't vary. It's an absolute reference, and remains B1.

Entering absolute references

Entering an absolute reference is easy. Simply insert $ in front of each formula component which won't change.

The correct version of the VAT formula in F3 would therefore be:

=E3*$B$1

R1C1 referencing

A1 is the referencing method which Excel 2002 uses by default (and which has been used throughout this book).

Excel 2002 can also make use of an older, alternative style of referencing cells (called the 'R1C1' method) by which both columns and rows are numbered. It has the advantage that the distinction between absolute and relative referencing is easier to understand. Its disadvantage is that it is not as brief as the A1 method.

Relative and absolute R1C1 referencing

In R1C1 style, Excel 2002 indicates absolute references as per the following example:

R2C2   the equivalent of $B$2 in A1 style

In other words, cell location is defined with an 'R' followed by a row number and a 'C' followed by a column number.

On the other hand, R1C1 relative references are enclosed in square brackets. Thus, if the active cell is B5, the relative cell reference R[1]C[1] refers to the cell one row down and one column to the right (i.e. C6).

Implementing R1C1 referencing

Pull down the Tools menu and click Options. Now do the following:

Activate the General tab

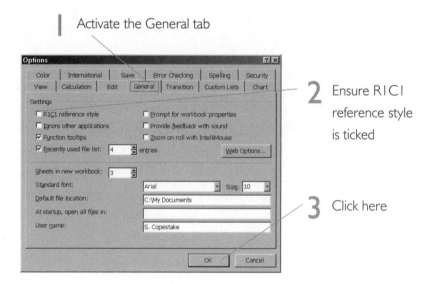

2 Ensure R1C1 reference style is ticked

3 Click here

Naming cells

An alternative way to reference cells is to give them a 'name' or identifier which describes the contents. Naming cells is a much more user-friendly technique than working with cell coordinates.

Defining names with the Name box

The easiest way to define names for cells is to use the Name box on the Formula Bar. Select the cell(s) you want to name, then do the following:

Names (it doesn't matter if they're lower or upper case) may be up to 255 characters long. The following rules apply:

- *The 1st character must be a letter or underscore: _*

- *Other characters may be any sequence of letters, digits, underscores and full stops (but not spaces)*

- *Separators must be either an underscore or full stop i.e. to apply VAT Rate as a name, you'd type in VAT_Rate*

Click here

You should note that you can't make use of standard cell references e.g.:

B2

H$12

R3C4

as names.

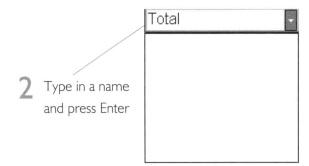

2 Type in a name and press Enter

The Name box is an effective shortcut to applying and inserting names. However, you can also use a more comprehensive menu route to:

- define and apply new names

- apply existing names

- delete names

- substitute already defined names for cell references, either in selected cells or globally

- paste names into the Formula Bar

Defining/applying names – the menu route

Do the following:

To delete a name, select it in the Define Names dialog and click Delete.

| Select one or more cells

2 Pull down the Insert menu and choose Name, Define

3 Now carry out step 4 OR 5 below. Finally, perform step 6:

4 Type in a new name

You can name formulas. In step 5, type in a name. In the Refers to box, type = followed by the formula. Click OK.

To use the named formula, press F2 in the relevant cell. Pull down the Insert menu and click Name, Paste. In the Paste Name dialog, double-click the formula.

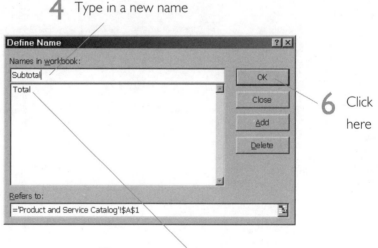

6 Click here

5 Click an existing name

Substituting names in formulas

You can have Excel 2002 automatically replace normal cell references in formulas with the appropriate pre-defined names.

The illustration below should clarify the need for this:

	A	B	C	D	E	F	G	H
1	VAT rate=	17.50%						
2		Product	Unit Price	Units Used	Amount due	VAT		
3		Widgets	£0.07	425	£29.75	£5.21		
4		Nuts	£0.13	246	£31.98			
5		Bolts	£0.08	380	£30.40			
6								
7								
8								
9								
10								
11								
12		Total amount due =	£92.13					
13								
14								
15								
16								
17								

Sheet6 / Sheet5 / **Sheet4** / Sheet1 / Sheet2 / Sheet3 /

The example shown here is a particularly simple one; name substitution comes into its own in large worksheets.

C12 contains this formula:

=SUM(E3:E5)

which totals E3, E4 and E5. If, however, these cells have had names allocated to them (e.g. Widget_total, Nut_total and Bolt_total), then it makes sense to adjust the formula in C12 accordingly. Fortunately, you can have Excel 2002 do this for you.

If you want to limit the swap to a single cell, select it and one other which contains no formulas.

Substituting names for references
Do ONE of the following:

1 Select the cells which contain the formulas whose references you want converted to the relevant names

2 Click any one cell in the worksheet if you want *all* formula references converted to the relevant names

Now carry out the additional procedures on page 78.

Now pull down the Insert menu and click Name, Apply. Carry out the following additional steps:

3 Click one or more names

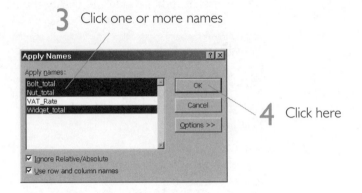

4 Click here

The end result:

Excel 2002 has inserted the relevant names into the formula

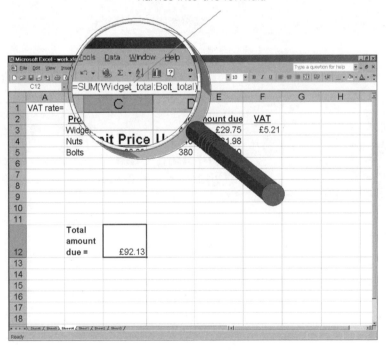

Pasting names

Excel 2002 lets you paste names directly into the Formula Bar while you're in the process of entering a formula.

Select the cell into which you want to insert the formula. Activate the Formula Bar by clicking in it. Begin the formula by typing:

=

You can 'toggle' between reference types as you work with formulas. **Click in the formula bar, select a reference and press F4 repeatedly.**

Now pull down the Insert menu and do the following:

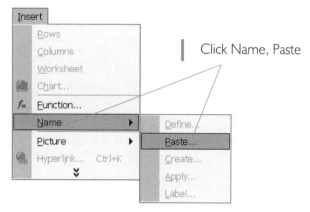

Click Name, Paste

2 Click a name

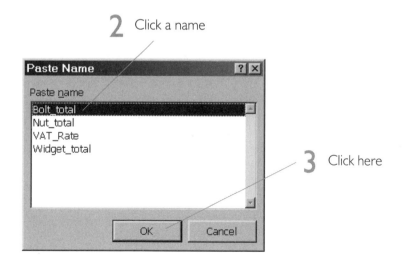

3 Click here

Cell reference operators

We've already encountered one cell reference operator: the colon. This is known as the Range operator and is used to define the rectangular block of cells formed between the two cell references which it separates. For example:

A5:E7

defines the block of cells which begins with A5 and ends with E7.

However, there are two other reference operators. Look at the next illustration:

With Intersection operators, the defining ranges must overlap. If they don't, Excel 2002 returns an error message complete with Smart Tag:

Click here

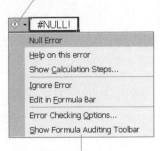

Make a choice e.g. click Help on this error for on-line assistance, or Show Calculation Steps to launch the Formula Evaluator

	A	B	C	D	E
1					
2		Qtr1	Qtr2	Qtr3	Qtr4
3		8000	10000	15000	12000
4		9000	11000	17000	13000
5		10000	12000	19000	14000
6					
7	Quarter 3 sales for 2000-2001=				51000
8	Quarter 3 sales for 1999=				17000

E7 contains this formula:

=SUM(D3,D4,D5)

The comma is known as the Union operator; it combines multiple references into one. In this case, the formula is totalling separate cells which could also be expressed as: D3:D5. However, this need not be the case. For instance, it could show: A3,B5,E8…

E8 contains the following formula:

=SUM(B4:E4 D3:D5)

The space separating the two ranges is known as the Intersection operator. The formula returns the cell at the intersection of B4:E4 and D3:D5 – in other words, D4.

Functions

In this chapter, you'll learn how to make your formulas much more effective by inserting functions and then editing them. Excel 2002 has a very large number of inbuilt functions which perform specialised calculations for wide-ranging applications e.g. statistical, mathematical, financial, etc. You'll learn how to utilise some of the most frequently used functions (including HYPERLINK, which inserts links to other worksheets/ documents, even those on intranets or the Internet), experience which can easily be carried across to Excel's more advanced functions.

You'll also discover how to use functions on-the-fly (by reference to Excel 2002's Status bar) and how to carry out sort operations.

Covers

Chapter Six

Functions – an overview

Use the functions explored in this chapter as examples: they should give you a good idea of how to apply other functions.

Functions are pre-defined tools which accomplish specific tasks. These tasks are often calculations; occasionally, however, they're more generalised (e.g. some functions simply return dates and/or times). In effect, functions replace one or more formulas.

Excel provides a special dialog to help ensure that you enter functions correctly. This is useful for the following reasons:

*   Excel 2002 provides so many functions, it's very convenient to apply (and amend) them from a centralised source: the Insert Function dialog

*   the Insert Function dialog ensures the functions are entered with the correct syntax

Functions can only be used in formulas, and are always followed by bracketed arguments.

You can use a shortcut (Excel calls this AutoCalculate) to total a cell range.
Select the range. Refer to the Status bar at the base of the screen; Excel displays the total:

Recognising functions

The following are examples of often-used functions:

SUM	Adds together a range of numbers
AVERAGE	Finds the average of a range of numbers
MAX	Finds the largest number in a range
MIN	Finds the smallest number in a range
LOOKUP	Compares a specified value with a specified cell range and returns a value
IF	Verifies if a condition is true or false, and acts accordingly

Some of the above are explored later in the chapter.

Sum=39000

You can use other simple functions in AutoCalculate.
Select a range. Right-click over the Status bar, then do the following:

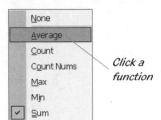

Click a function

Working with functions

Excel 2002 organises its functions under convenient headings e.g.:

- *Financial*
- *Date & Time*
- *Statistical*
- *Text*

Functions can only be used in formulas.

Inserting a function

1 At the relevant juncture while inserting a formula, refer to the Formula bar and click this button: f_x

2 Type in a brief description of the function you want and click here

If you know the function you want and it's fairly simple, you can enter it directly into a cell (preceded by =). When you do this, Excel often launches a ToolTip e.g.:

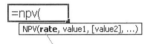

A helpful ToolTip – clicking an argument or function often launches HELP

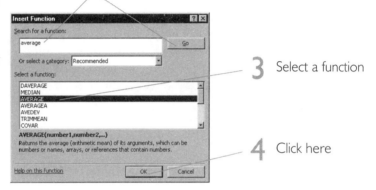

3 Select a function

4 Click here

5 Enter the function arguments

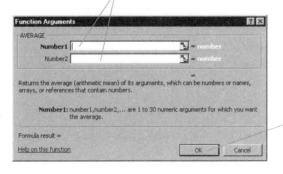

To edit an existing function, click the relevant cell. Press F2. Make the necessary changes and press Enter.

You can also type functions directly into a formula but only if you know the syntax. It's often easier to use the Insert Function dialog route.

6 Click here

The SUM function

You can use a shortcut here. Pre-select the cells you want to total before you carry out step 1. For instance, if you select B3:F6 and then click the AutoSum button, Excel 2002 inserts all relevant totals.

The SUM function totals specified cells. You can insert a SUM function by using the Insert Function dialog – see page 83. However, you can also use a useful shortcut – AutoSum – to total adjacent cells automatically. Look at the next illustration:

	A	B	C	D	E	F
1						
2		Qtr1	Qtr2	Qtr3	Qtr4	
3		8000	10000	15000	12000	
4		9000	11000	17000	13000	
5		10000	12000	19000	14000	

To total the range B3:E3 in F3, click cell F3. Now refer to the Standard toolbar and do the following:

| Click the AutoSum button

For more information on specific functions, enter 'function' in the Ask-a-Question box in Excel's main screen and press Enter. In the list, click Examples of commonly used formulas.

Excel 2002 surrounds the cells it believes should be included in the SUM function with a dotted line:

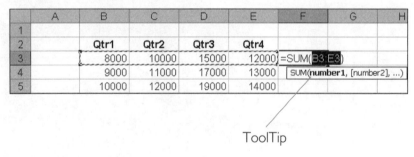

	A	B	C	D	E	F	G	H
1								
2		Qtr1	Qtr2	Qtr3	Qtr4			
3		8000	10000	15000	12000	=SUM(B3:E3)		
4		9000	11000	17000	13000	SUM(**number1**, [number2], ...)		
5		10000	12000	19000	14000			

ToolTip

Click a function for more details

Amend the formula entry in F3, if necessary. Then press Enter; Excel 2002 inserts the SUM function.

The LOOKUP function

LOOKUP compares a value you set (the Look-Up value) with the first row or column in a Look-Up table. If it finds a matching value, it returns it in the cell you specify. If it doesn't, it returns the largest value in the table which is the same as or less than the Look-Up value.

LOOKUP can also work with text values and/or names.

Alternatively, if the Look-Up value is smaller than all the values in the Look-Up table, LOOKUP returns an error:

The values in the Look-Up table must be in ascending order. If they're not, you can rectify this. Select the values. Pull down the Data menu and click Sort. In the Sort by section in the Sort dialog, make sure Ascending is selected. Finally, click OK.

Click the Smart Tag – in the menu, select an option e.g. Help on this error, or Show Calculation Steps to launch the Formula Evaluator

The Look-Up value

	A	B	C	D	E	F
1						
2						
3	Monthly lease rates per £1000 borrowed					
4	Years	Rates				
5	1	£22.50				
6	2	£26.58				
7	3	£47.31				
8	4	£49.22		Lease term in years=		50
9	5	£89.08		Lease value=		

The Look-Up table

Here, a Look-Up table and value have been established. In this instance, names have also been applied, for convenience:

- the table (B5:B9) is Lease_Table

- the value (F8) is Lease_Term

It only remains to enter and define the LOOKUP function – see page 86 for how to do this.

Using LOOKUP

1 Select the relevant cell (in the example on page 85, F9)

2 Follow step 1 on page 83

3 Follow steps 2-3 on page 83. In step 2, type in 'lookup' (omit the quotes); in step 3, select LOOKUP

4 Follow step 4 on page 83

5 Double-click lookup_value,array

Re step 6 – in this example, names have been entered since they've been applied to the relevant cells.

6 Follow step 5 on page 83. In Lookup_value, type 'Lease_Term'; in Array, type 'Lease_Table' (omit the quotes). Click OK

The inserted formula

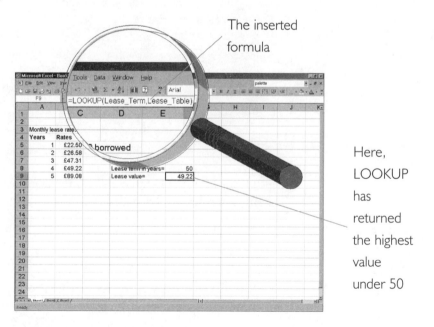

Here, LOOKUP has returned the highest value under 50

The IF function

The IF function checks whether a specified condition is TRUE or FALSE and carries out one or more specified actions accordingly.

Look at the next illustration:

An advanced tip – you can 'nest' IF functions within themselves (up to a total of 7 times) by using brackets within brackets. For more help with this, enter 'IF function' (no quotes) into the Ask-a-Question box in Excel's main screen and press Enter. In the list, select IF worksheet function. See Example 3 in the HELP text.

	A	B	C	D
1				
2				
3		**Name**	**Amount Spent**	**Discount**
4				
5		Brierley	1,280	
6		Jones	1,020	
7		Mitchell	570	
8		Harrison	1150	
9		Wood	870	

Here, Individual customer discounts need to be calculated in D5:D9. Each discount in D5:D9 depends on the following conditions:

- if the amount a customer has spent is greater than or equal to £1000, then the discount is 20%

- if the amount a customer has spent is less than £1000 then the discount is 10%

Using the IF Function

1 Select the cell you want to host the function – in the case of the example above, D5 (initially)

2 Follow step 1 on page 83

3 Follow steps 2-3 on page 83. In step 2, type in 'logical test' (omit the quotes); in step 3, select IF. Click OK

4 Enter the 'logical test'

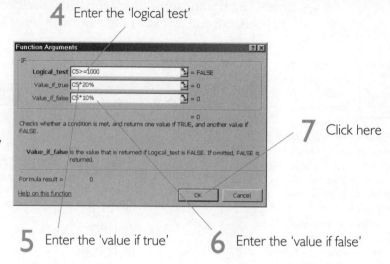

See the Glossary below for an explanation of the terms used in steps 4–6.

7 Click here

The IF function uses comparison operators.

5 Enter the 'value if true'

6 Enter the 'value if false'

Glossary

Logical test	The condition. In this instance: C5>=1000 (i.e. the contents of C5 must be greater than or equal to 1000)
Value if true	The action to be taken if the condition is met. In this instance: C5*20% (i.e. the contents of C5 are multiplied by 20%)
Value if false	The action to be taken if the condition isn't met. In this instance: C5*10% (i.e. the contents of C5 are multiplied by 10%)

The end result:

Name	Amount Spent	Discount
Brierley	1,280	256
Jones	1,020	204
Mitchell	570	57
Harrison	1150	230
Wood	870	87

The IF function has been inserted into D5, and extrapolated into D6:D9 with AutoFill

The HYPERLINK function

You can use the HYPERLINK function to insert links to documents on:

- network servers

- Intranets/the Internet

- local hard disks

Hyperlinks can also include pointers to:

- specific cells or ranges in Excel 2002 worksheets

- Word 2002 bookmarks

You can also insert hyperlinks via a more conventional method.

Right-click the text or picture you want to serve as a hyperlink. In the menu, click Hyperlink. On the left of the Insert Hyperlink dialog, select a hyperlink type (e.g. Existing File or Web Page). On the right, select a file/worksheet, or type in a Web/email address, as appropriate. Click OK.

Using the HYPERLINK function

1 Select the cell you want to host the function

2 Follow step 1 on page 83

3 Type in 'hyperlink' (no quotes) and click Go

4 Click HYPERLINK then OK

Re step 5 – to include specific cells in the link, carry out the following procedure:

- surround the address details in square brackets
- add the range reference later

For example, to link to cells 'B3:C6' in the worksheet 'Annual' in the workbook 'Accounts.xls' stored at www.commerce.com, type (without line breaks or spaces):

[http://www.commerce. com/accounts.xls] Annual!B3:C6

Re step 5 – to link to a Word 2002 bookmark, type the bookmark name immediately after the bracketed address e.g.:

[c:\mywork\report.doc] bookmark

(Include no line breaks or spaces.)

To select a cell containing a hyperlink, Ctrl+click it.

5 Enter the hyperlink address

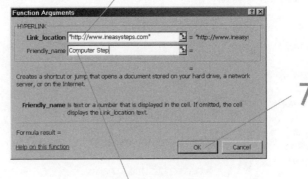

7 Click here

6 Enter the text you want to display in the cell

Here, B4 hosts a hyperlink to the Computer Step Web site – to activate the hyperlink, click it

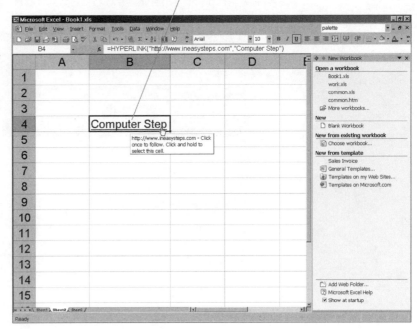

Using speech recognition

Dictating data into Excel 2002 provides a valuable alternative way to input it – you can also use speech recognition to enter commands etc.

First, you'll carry out a custom install, to install speech recognition for use with Excel. Then you'll 'train' the software, so it's set up for your voice and dictating conditions. You'll go on to dictate content into Excel 2002 and have it turned into on-screen data or text. When errors occur, you'll correct them with the mouse and keyboard (in the usual way) or dictate the replacement.

Finally, you'll launch menus, toolbar buttons and dialogs with dedicated voice commands.

Covers

Chapter Seven

Preparing to use speech recognition

To use speech recognition, you need the following:

- *a high-quality headset, preferably with USB (Universal Serial Bus) support and gain adjustment*

- *a minimum chip speed of 400 MHz (slower chips make dictation extremely laborious)*

- *a minimum of 128 Mb of RAM*

- *Windows 98 (or NT 4.0) or later*

- *Internet Explorer 5.0 (or later)*

For more information on requirements, visit (no spaces or line breaks):

http://Excel.microsoft.com/ assistance/2002/articles/ oSpeechRequirements_aw. htm

If you run speech recognition in less than optimal conditions, the results may well be poor.

Your use of speech recognition will benefit from repeated training. Click the Tools button on the Language Bar and select Training. Complete the wizard which launches.

Installing/running speech recognition

If you haven't already done so, you must first run a custom install. In Control Panel, double-click Add/Remove Programs. Select Microsoft Office XP... Click Add/Remove, then Add or Remove Features, Next. Double-click Office Shared Features, then Alternative User Input. Select Speech then the type of installation you need. Click Update.

Preparing speech recognition

Before you can dictate into Excel 2002, you have to adjust your microphone and carry out a brief 'training' procedure to acclimatise Excel to the sound of your voice:

1   Choose Tools, Speech, Speech Recognition

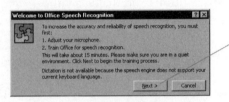

2   Click Next to begin the training process

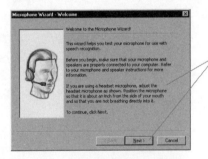

3   Adjust your microphone in line with the instructions then click Next

4   Read out the sentence shown then click Next. Complete the rest of the wizard – it should take about 15 minutes

Dictating data

To start or end speech recognition, choose Tools, Speech, Speech Recognition.

Starting to dictate

| If the microphone isn't already turned on, click here

To get the best out of speech recognition, you need to carry out the following:

- *keep your environment as quiet as possible*
- *keep the microphone in the same position relative to your mouth*
- *run the training wizard as often as possible*
- *pronounce words clearly but don't pause between them or between individual letters – only pause at the end of your train of thought*
- *turn off the microphone when not in use (by repeating step 1)*

2 The Language bar expands – click Dictation

3 Begin dictating. Initially, Excel inserts a blue bar on the screen – the data/text appears as soon as it's recognised

For the best results, use speech recognition in conjunction with mouse and keyboard use.

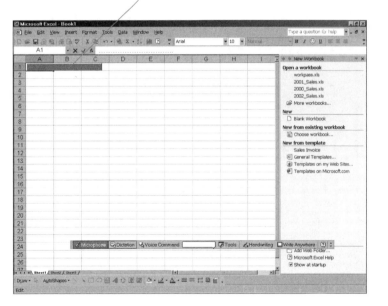

4 When you've finished, follow the procedure in the HOT TIP

Entering voice commands

You can switch to Voice Command by saying 'Voice Command', or dictation by saying 'Dictation'.

| Follow step 1 on page 93

2 Click Voice Command

Commands you speak appear in the following Language bar field:

Task Pane

For more details of voice commands, see the HELP topic 'Getting started with speech recognition'.

3 Issue the appropriate command using the following as guides:

- to launch the File menu say 'file' or 'file menu' (to select a menu entry say the name)
- to open the Font dialog say 'font' (to select a typeface, say the name)
- to close a dialog say 'OK'
- to select a toolbar button, say the name
- to launch the Task Pane, say 'Task Pane'

Correcting errors

If the Language Bar isn't visible or minimised on the Taskbar, go to Control Panel. Double-click Text Services. In the dialog, click Language Bar. Select Show the Language bar on the desktop. Click OK twice.

| Replace wrong text with corrections in the usual way

2 Or select the error with your mouse. In Dictation mode, say 'spelling mode'. Now spell out the substitution e.g. o-n-c-e

3 Or select the error with your mouse. In Dictation mode, say the corrected version

Re step 3 – it's best to correct phrases rather than individual words.

Cell errors and auditing

Given the eventual size of most worksheets, problems sometimes occur when Excel 2002 is unable to evaluate a formula. Error messages appear when this happens – here, you'll learn how to deal with them. Messages are shown 'on-the-fly', with reference to specific examples and also with the appropriate corrections.

Excel 2002 supplies a set of auditing tools. You'll learn how to use these to track dependent and precedent cells and to trace errors, so you can feel confident about creating and troubleshooting your own formulas. You'll also use a dialog route to pinpoint cells which are in conflict with formulas and discover a new way to launch the Watch Window.

Finally, you'll insert comments into cells, and edit or delete them subsequently.

Covers

Chapter Eight

Cell errors

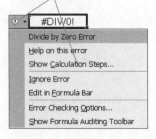

The following table shows details of some of the common Excel 2002 error messages (they're shown in action in the illustration below).

#DIV/0!   In this instance, this error is caused by an attempt to divide 2.5 by zero. Theoretically this should generate infinity. In practice any such value is too big, even for a computer, and the calculation is suppressed

#N/A   This means that No value is Available. The LOOKUP argument (B8, B5:D6) should refer to cell D8 instead of B8; B8 – since it contains text – is incorrect

#NAME?   Excel 2002 fails to recognise the Name of the function 'IS', which has been incorrectly typed for 'IF'

#NULL!   This formula uses the intersection operator (a space) to locate the cell at the intersection of ranges B15:D15 and A16:A18. Since they don't intersect, Excel 2002 displays the error message

	A	B	C	D	D
1	(1)				
2		2.5	0	#DIV/0!	=B2/C2
3					
4	(2)				
5	Amount:	£0	£500	£1,000	1000
6	Discount:	0.0%	5.0%	10.0%	0.1
7					
8		Price =		£750	750
9		Discount Rate =		#N/A	=LOOKUP(B8, B5:D6)
10					
11	(3)				
12		-0.25		#NAME?	=IS(B12=0, "Zero", "Non-zero")
13					
14	(4)				
15		5	10	15	15
16	2				
17	4				
18	6			#NULL!	=B15:D15 A16:A18

The above error messages in action

Here are some additional error messages, and details of their causes:

#NUM!   This error value indicates problems with numbers. The first example of this error (see below) attempts to generate the value 100^{1000}, i.e. 100 multiplied by itself 1000 times. This is too large for the computer to store and so the calculation is suppressed

In the second example the attempt to calculate the square root (SQRT function) of a negative value is suppressed

#VALUE!   This error occurs when the data in a cell isn't appropriate for the operation, or the operation doesn't apply to the type of data. Here an attempt has been made to divide 'Text' by 50

The number of hash symbols varies according to the column size.

This error is not necessarily generated by a formula. In this case the number stored is simply too long for the cell width

The data/error messages are on the left of the illustration; the formulas which gave rise to the errors are on the right.

	A	B	C	D	D
20	(5)				
21		100	1000	#NUM!	=B21^C21
22		16		#NUM!	=SQRT(-B22)
23					
24	(6)				
25		Text	50	#VALUE!	=B25/C25
26					
27	(7)				
28				########	100000000
29					
30	(8)				
31		100			
32			50	2	=B31/C32

The examples on pages 96–98 are simple, practical illustrations of the causes of error messages. In practice, tracking down the origin of an error message is sometimes less than straightforward, because a single error may cause a proliferation of error values.
   (See pages 99–101 for tracking techniques.)

The final error message we'll discuss here is more complex:

#REF!   To generate this error requires another stage. On page 97, the formula in D32:

=B31/C32#

divides the contents of cell B31 by the contents of cell C32, initially producing the correct answer. However, if Excel can't locate one of the cells referred to (e.g. if B31 no longer exists because row 31 has been deleted), it displays this message

This process is demonstrated in the illustration below:

#REF! only appears if you've deleted the cell referred to by a formula; clearing the cell's contents (e.g. by selecting it and clicking Clear, Contents in the Edit menu) will, instead, produce '0'.

2 The formula has changed; the B31 component has been replaced by #REF! and C32 has now become C31

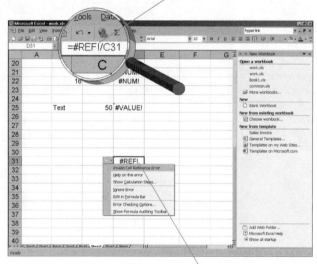

Some worksheet items can't be traced. These include:

• text boxes

• formulas which relate to the cell but which are in external workbooks that aren't currently open

Since row 31 has been deleted and the reference in the formula to B31 is invalid, Excel 2002 displays the error message (complete with Smart Tag)

Auditing tools

Auditing displays tracer arrows between cells. In order to make these arrows more visible, you may wish to hide worksheet gridlines.

Pull down the Tools menu and click Options. Activate the View tab; in the Window options section, deselect Gridlines. Finally, click OK.

Excel 2002 provides a variety of features you can use to ensure formulas work correctly. You can use the Formula Auditing toolbar to have Excel delineate cell relationships with arrows ('tracers'). In this way, if a formula returns an error message, you can track down which cell is misbehaving.

Cells which are referred to by a formula in another cell are called precedents. For example, if cell H26 has the formula:

$=M97$

M97 is a precedent.

Inserting precedent tracers

You can use the Formula Auditing Toolbar to launch the Watch Window. Click this button:

Click the cell whose precedents you want to display. Pull down the Tools menu and click Formula Auditing, Show Formula Auditing Toolbar. Now do the following:

Click here

Tracer arrows vanish if you change the formula they point to, insert rows/columns or delete/ move cells. To reinstate them, repeat step 1.

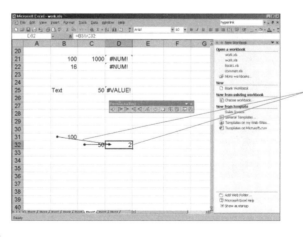

Precedent tracers – D32 (selected) hosts a formula whose precedents are B31 and C32

Before carrying out the procedures here, pull down the Tools menu and click Options. Activate the View tab; in the Objects section, ensure Show all is selected. Finally, click OK.

To remove all tracer arrows on the worksheet (e.g. when you've finished the audit, or perhaps to start again from a different cell), simply click this button:

in the Formula Auditing toolbar.

You can use a special dialog to facilitate error checking. Click this button in the Formula Auditing Toolbar:

In the Error Checking dialog, click Help on this error (for assistance), Show Calculation Steps (to launch the Formula Evaluator) or Edit in Formula Bar (followed by Resume when you've finished) to amend the errant formula in situ.

Before carrying out the procedures here, pull down the Tools menu and click Options. Activate the View tab; in the Objects section, ensure Show all is selected. Finally, click OK.

Cells which contain formulas referring to other cells are called dependents. For instance, if cell H6 has the formula:

=SUM(C6:D8)

H6 is a dependent cell (and the cells in the range C6:D8 are precedent cells – see page 99).

Inserting dependent tracers

Select a cell which is referred to in a formula. Pull down the Tools menu and click Formula Auditing, Show Formula Auditing Toolbar. Now do the following:

Click here

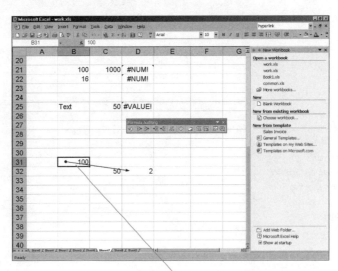

A dependent tracer – B31 (selected) is referenced by the formula in D32, and the tracer highlights this

Using the Error Tracer

The Error Tracer locates all cells affected by the error.

When a formula returns an error, you can use another auditing tool – the Error Tracer – to track it back to its source and then correct it.

Using the Error Tracer

Select a cell which contains an error value. Pull down the Tools menu and click Formula Auditing, Show Formula Auditing toolbar. Now do the following:

Before carrying out the procedures here, pull down the Tools menu and click Options. Activate the View tab; in the Objects section, ensure Show all is selected. Finally, click OK.

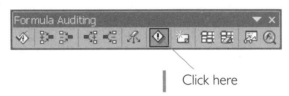

Click here

Excel 2002 flags all cells referred to by the incorrect formula in D25

Since tracer arrows disappear if you carry out certain actions, it's a good idea to print out the worksheet with the arrows, for reference.

If Excel beeps when you carry out a trace, it has either found all the relevant levels or you're trying to trace the wrong type of item.

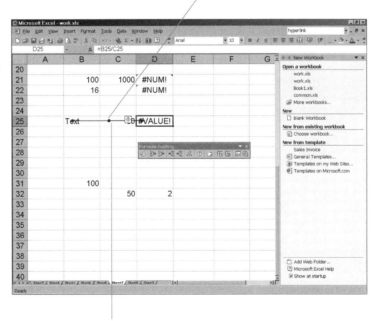

Note – if the error has multiple incorrect paths, Excel will only flag the first path. Repeat step 1

Always clear existing tracer arrows by clicking this button in the Formula Auditing toolbar:

before reusing the Error Tracer.

Working with comments

You can attach comments to cells. Once inserted, comments can be viewed or edited at will.

1. Inserting a comment

Select the relevant cell. Pull down the Insert menu and click Comment. Now do the following:

Red comment flag

Comment box

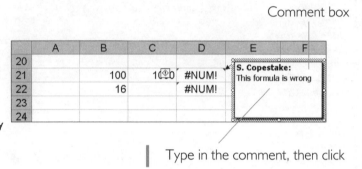

	A	B	C	D	E	F
20						
21		100	100	#NUM!	S. Copestake:
22		16		#NUM!	This formula is wrong
23						
24						

Type in the comment, then click outside the box

2. Editing a comment

Select the relevant cell (for how to recognise cells which contain comments, see the upper DON'T FORGET tip). Pull down the Insert menu and click Edit Comment. Now click inside the Comment box and amend the text as necessary. Click outside the box when you've finished.

3. Deleting a comment

Right-click any cell which contains a comment. Do the following:

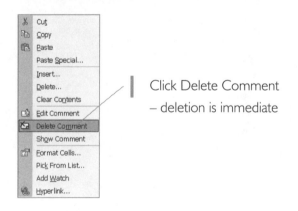

Click Delete Comment – deletion is immediate

Workbook security

Nowadays, especially with widespread Internet and intranet use, data security is increasingly an issue. However, Excel 2002 has very comprehensive security options.

First, you'll ensure your data is secure. You'll 'protect' cells, a technique which allows you to specify precisely which cells can and can't be amended. Then you'll protect specific cell ranges and specify precise details of which operations can be carried out. You'll also prevent unauthorised users from modifying workbook structure and resizing workbook windows.

Finally, you'll restrict access to your workbooks by allocating passwords, then reopen them and (if necessary) change the passwords.

Covers

Chapter Nine

Protecting cells

Individual cells can be protected so that they can't be amended, resized, deleted or moved. This is a two-stage process:

1.   'Unlocking' those cells which you'll want to amend *after* the host worksheet has been protected (you won't be able to modify any of the other cells)

2.   Protecting the worksheet

Unlocking cells

Select the cells you want to unlock. Pull down the Format menu and do the following:

In summary, Excel 2002 lets you protect your data on various levels:

- *you can protect entire workbooks from being viewed and amended*
- *you can protect specific cell ranges, or (if you're using Windows 2000) you can restrict access to them to specific users*
- *(to a lesser extent) you can protect specific cells*

See pages 33-34 for another way to secure your data: digital signatures.

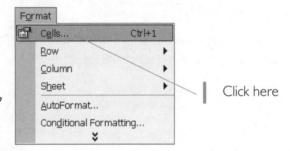

1 Click here

2 Ensure the Protection tab is activated

If you select the Hidden field, the formula(s) in the selected cell(s) will be hidden (provided you've protected the host worksheet) and won't appear in the Formula bar.

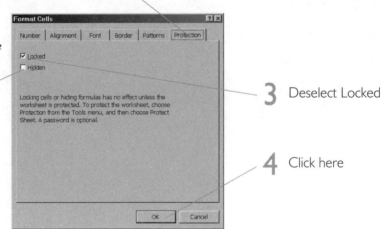

3 Deselect Locked

4 Click here

...cont'd

If you want to modify cell protection, pull down the Tools menu and click Protection, Unprotect Sheet. If necessary, type in the relevant password in the Unprotect Sheet dialog and click OK. Then select the relevant cells. Press Ctrl+1. Activate the Protection tab in the Format Cells dialog; select or deselect Locked, as appropriate. Click OK.

Finally, perform steps 1– 4 again.

Running a macro which attempts to carry out a protected operation makes it fail.

You can have Excel 2002 warn you when you're about to open a workbook containing macros (small, independent programs – see Chapter 16) which might contain harmful viruses.

Pull down the Tools menu and click Macro, Security. Activate the Security Level tab. Select a protection level and click OK.

Note that Excel can't actually verify whether viruses are present; it can only warn you of the possibility...

Protecting the host worksheet

1 Pull down the tools menu and select Protection, Protect Sheet

2 Tick this

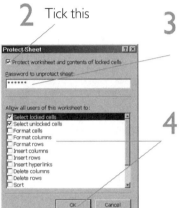

3 Optional – enter a password (used if you want to unprotect the sheet – see the HOT TIP)

4 Tick those aspects you want enabled for all users of the worksheet, then click OK

The effects of cell protection

When you've protected cells, the following results apply:

1. Any attempt to overwrite/edit a locked cell produces a special message:

2. When a locked cell is selected, certain menu commands are greyed out

3. If a locked cell is selected, pressing Tab will move the cursor to the next locked cell (the movement is from top to bottom, and left to right). Pressing Shift+Tab reverses the direction

Protecting cell ranges

You can protect specific ranges within worksheets.

Immediately after the procedures here, pull down the Tools menu and click Protection, Protect Sheet. Or click the Protect Sheet button before step 5. In the Protect Sheet dialog, tick Protect worksheet and contents of locked cells. Optional – enter a password if you want to prevent unauthorised unprotection of the sheet. In the main body of the dialog, tick those aspects (e.g. Format Cells or Insert Hyperlinks) you want enabled for all users of the worksheet.

Finally, click OK.

Setting up range protection

1 Pull down the Tools menu and click Protection, Allow Users to Edit Ranges

2 Click here

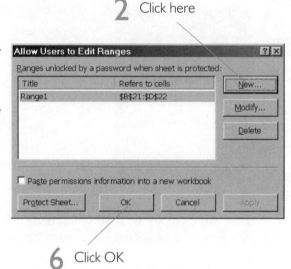

6 Click OK

3 Name and specify a range

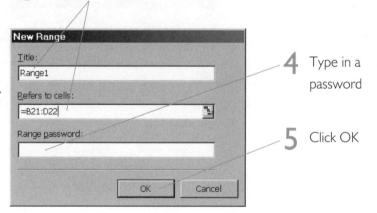

4 Type in a password

5 Click OK

If you're using Windows 2000, you can specify which users can amend which cells.

Go to the protected worksheet in the relevant workbook. Pull down the Tools menu and select Protection, Unprotect Sheet. Enter any necessary password and click OK. Carry out step 1. In the Allow Users to Edit Ranges dialog, select a pre-specified range and click Modify. Select Permissions. Make the necessary changes and then confirm.

Protecting workbook structure

You can 'protect' the following workbook aspects:

To remove protection from the active workbook, pull down the Tools menu and click Protection, Unprotect Workbook. If necessary, type in the relevant password and click OK.

- structure (this prevents worksheets from being deleted, renamed, copied/moved or inserted)

- windows (this prevents workbook windows from being resized, moved or closed)

When the above are active, the relevant menu commands are greyed out.

Protecting an entire workbook

Pull down the Tools menu and do the following:

Running a macro which attempts to carry out an operation which can't be performed in a protected workbook makes the macro fail.

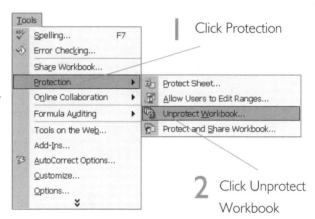

Click Protection

2 Click Unprotect Workbook

3 Tick either or both of these

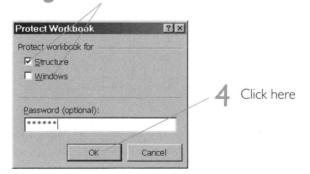

4 Click here

Password-protecting workbooks

You can protect your workbooks by:

• allocating an 'Open' password

• allocating a 'Modify' password

The first allows users to open the associated workbook but prevents them from saving changes *under the existing filename.* The second, on the other hand, allows users to modify and save the workbook.

Passwords are case-sensitive, and can be up to 15 characters long. They can be any combination of letters, numbers, spaces and other symbols.

You impose passwords in the course of carrying out a Save As operation.

Allocating a password

Pull down the File menu and click Save As. Now carry out steps 1–5 below:

If you lose or forget the password, you won't be able to recover the **workbook!**

Repeat step 3 as necessary, until you locate the relevant folder.

2 Click here. In the drop-down list, click a drive

5 Click Tools

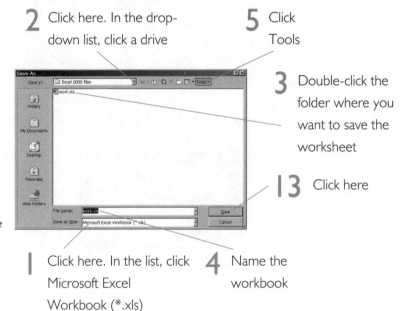

3 Double-click the folder where you want to save the worksheet

13 Click here

1 Click here. In the list, click Microsoft Excel Workbook (*.xls)

4 Name the workbook

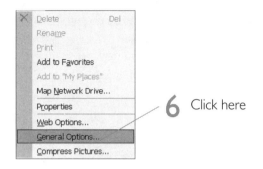

6 Click here

7 Type in an Open password

Follow step 7, step 8 or steps 7 and 8, as appropriate.

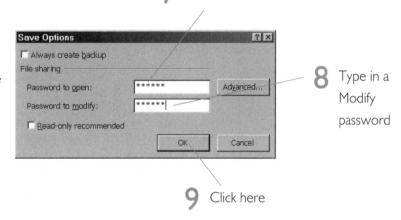

8 Type in a Modify password

9 Click here

10 Reiterate the Open password

If you carried out step 8, Excel 2002 launches another Confirm Password dialog after step 11. Reiterate your Modify password, then click OK.

Finally, carry out steps 12-13.

11 Click here

12 Finally, carry out step 13 on the facing page

Opening protected workbooks

Once passwords have been allocated to a file, you can modify or remove them.

With the file open, pull down the File menu and click Save As. Carry out the procedures on pages 108-109 to allocate one or more new passwords. (To remove passwords, leave the relevant fields blank in steps 7 and 8.)

Opening a password-protected workbook

| Follow steps 3-4 on page 67

2 If you allocated an Open password, enter it here

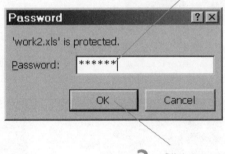

3 Click here

If you enter the wrong Open or Modify password, Excel 2002 launches a message. Do the following:

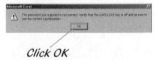

Click OK

Now repeat the relevant procedures. When you re-enter the password(s), however, ensure that:

* *the Caps Lock key is not active*

* *you type in the password with the correct capitalisation (passwords are case-sensitive)*

If the workbook you're opening has had a Modify password allocated to it, Excel launches a further dialog. Carry out steps 4-5 below to open the workbook with the ability to modify it and save changes under the original name. Alternatively, carry out step 6 alone to open the workbook as a 'read-only' file (i.e. any amendments you make subsequently must be saved under a different name).

4 Type in the Modify password

Password   ? X

'work2.xls' is reserved by S. Copestake

Enter password for write access, or open read only.

Password: ******

OK

Cancel

Read Only

5 Click here

6 Click Read Only

Data analysis

Entering data is one thing but you'll also want to look for trends. Luckily, predicting the effects of changing data is one of Excel's strong-points.

In this chapter, you'll explore how to preview changes to selected data values and gauge the effect on the overall data pattern, and how to extrapolate predictions based on current figures and formulas. You'll also switch to manual (rather than automatic) calculation, a useful technique in especially large worksheets, and apply PivotTables and PivotCharts to reformulate data dynamically.

Covers

Chapter Ten

Data analysis – an overview

Note that this excerpt contains the following formulas:

Cell	Formula
D6	D4*D5
D10	D6-D8

Some of the examples later in this chapter will make use of these.

Look at the following worksheet extract:

	A	B	C	D
1				
2		**Video Rentals**		
3				
4		Rental Price=		£2.00
5		Number of Rentals=		250
6		Total Income=		£500
7				
8		Total Costs=		£200
9				
10		Net Profit=		£300
11				

By default, Excel 2002 recalculates formulas in dependent cells when the values in precedent cells are changed. If the network of dependent formulas is large, you may have to wait for the update to finish. This is frustrating if you wish to change several values and have to wait after each one while the rest of the worksheet is recalculated.

To have formulas calculated manually instead, see the margin icons on page 113.

Here, we have a simple worksheet which calculates the Net Profit based on several data values relating to the renting out of videos.

You should bear the following in mind:

Total Income (D6)　　= Rental Price (D4) x Number of Rentals (D5)

Net Profit (D10)　　= Total Income (D6) – Total Costs (D8)

See the HOT TIP for details of formulas contained in the extract.

Later topics in this chapter will explore various techniques which allow you to interpolate data into the extract conveniently and easily. Once interpolated, changes to data values will ripple through the extract automatically, and can be viewed (and later discarded, if required) at will.

Using Goal Seek

Refer back to the illustration on page 112 and consider the following:

Let's suppose we need to know the number of video rentals necessary to break even. In other words, we want to find out how many rentals are necessary to meet the total costs, thereby ensuring that the net profit is £0. In the case of a simple example like this, you could arrive at the correct figure manually, by trial and error, without too much time and effort. However, more complex worksheets would clearly make this approach impracticable.

Instead, however, you can use a Goal Seek What-If test.

Applying a Goal Seek What-If test

First, select the cell which contains the formula you need to resolve (in this instance, D10). Pull down the Tools menu and do the following:

To turn on manual calculation globally, pull down the Tools menu and click Options. In the Options dialog, activate the Calculation tab. Select Manual in the Calculation section.
Finally, click OK.
(For how to activate manual calculation in respect of open worksheets only, see the tips below.)

To invoke manual calculation within all open worksheets, simply press F9.

To invoke manual calculation within the active worksheet only, press Shift+F9.

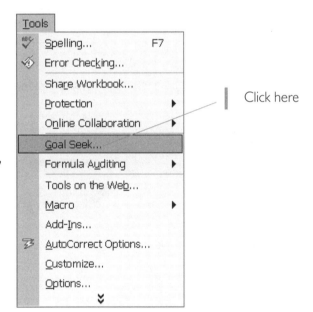

Click here

Now carry out the following steps:

2 Type in the target value (in this case, 0)

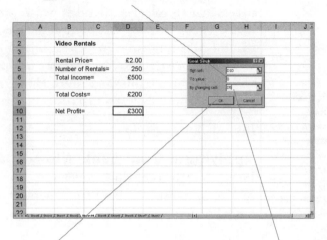

4 Click here   **3** Type in the reference of the cell you want to change (in this case, D5)

Excel 2002 has calculated the What-If value...

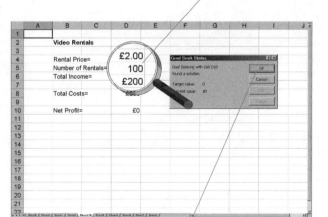

HOT TIP

Re step 5 – click the Cancel button instead if you don't want the result of the Goal Seek inserted permanently into your worksheet.

The ability not to implement the Goal Seek results makes this a useful technique for exploring alternatives.

5 Click here to update the worksheet

One-variable data tables

Irrespective of whether data tables have changed, they automatically recalculate when you recalculate the host worksheet.

You can, however, speed the process up. Pull down the Tools menu and click Options. In the Options dialog, select the Calculation tab. Tick Automatic except tables. Click OK.

Please refer back to the illustration on page 112 and consider the following additional hypothesis:

Let's suppose we wanted to know how the Net Profit would change when the Rental Price is changed. We could do this using the simple What-If technique of varying the Rental Price and recording the corresponding change in the Net Profit. However, it would be necessary to repeat this for as many separate rental price values as we wished to test.

A much simpler and quicker route is to use a one-variable data table.

Applying a one-variable data table

Carry out the following steps:

2 Type in the necessary formula (but see the tips on the left)

Re step 2 – enter the formula which returns the Net Profit. Here, you simply refer to the relevant cell:

=D10

	A	B	C	D	E	F	G	H
1								
2		Video Rentals				Rental Price	Net Profit	
3							£300	
4		Rental Price=		£2.00		£1.00		
5		Number of Rentals=		250		£1.25		
6		Total Income=		£500		£1.50		
7						£1.75		
8		Total Costs=		£200		£2.00		
9						£2.25		
10		Net Profit=		£300		£2.50		
11								
12								
13								
14								
15								
16								
17								
18								
19								

Sheet5 / Sheet4 / Sheet1 / Sheet2 / Sheet10 / Sheet6 / Sheet9 \ Sheet8 / Sheet7

Re step 2 – if you insert values in a column, the formula cell must be in the row above the first value, and one cell to the right. If you type in values in a row, however, it must be in the column to the left of the first value, and one cell below.

One-variable tables will only work if these conditions are met.

In a row or column (in this case, F4:F10), type in the values for which you want to generate alternatives

Now select the table. Pull down the Data menu and click Table.
Then carry out the following steps:

You must select
both columns
or rows (but
not the
headings).

The selected table

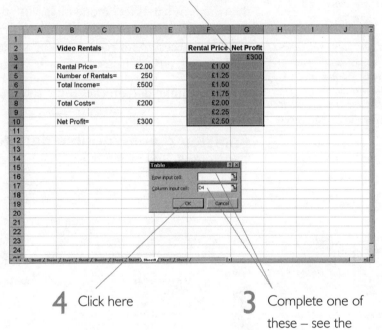

Re step 3 –
complete the
Column input
cell field if you
created a
columnar table, the Row
input cell field if you created
a row-based table.

You should enter the
reference of the input cell
for which the initial table
values (in this case, F4:F10)
are to be substituted. Here,
enter 'D4' (omit the quotes).

4 Click here

3 Complete one of
these – see the
HOT TIP

Rental Price	Net Profit
	£300
£1.00	50
£1.25	112.5
£1.50	175
£1.75	237.5
£2.00	300
£2.25	362.5
£2.50	425

The
completed
one-variable
table

Two-variable data tables

Please refer back to the illustration on page 112 and consider the following:

So far, the examples we've examined have been fairly simple. Suppose, however, that we need to know how the Net Profit would vary relative to *both* of the following:

- the Rental Price

- the Number of Rentals

Excel 2002 has a technique we can use to extrapolate this, too, despite the increased complexity of the operation. We need to use a two-variable data table.

Applying a two-variable data table

Construct the appropriate table – refer to the illustration below as a guide. Then do the following:

Re step 1 – the correct cell reference in this example is F4.

1 Select the cell at the intersection of the row containing the first input values and the column containing the second

	D	E	F	G	H	I	J	K
1								
2			Rental			Net Profit		
3			Price		Number of Rentals			
4	£2.00		£300.00	100	125	150	175	200
5	250		£1.00					
6	£500		£1.25					
7			£1.50					
8	£200		£1.75					
9			£2.00					
10	£300		£2.25					
11			£2.50					

Re step 2 – in this example, the input categories are the following:

- *rental price*

- *number of rentals*

Therefore, the cell which relates to them is D10 (i.e. Net Profit) and the formula is:

=D10

2 Press F2. Type in the formula which relates to the two input categories and press Enter

Now select the table. This stage is crucial. The selection must include:

- the formula cell (F4 in the example on page 117)

- the row and column of input data (F5:F11 and G4:K4 in the example on page 117)

- the empty body of the table (G5:K11 in the example on page 117)

Pull down the Data menu and click Table. Now do the following:

Re step 3 – in the current example, the cell which relates to the number of rentals is D5.

3 Type in the reference for the cell which relates to the number of rentals

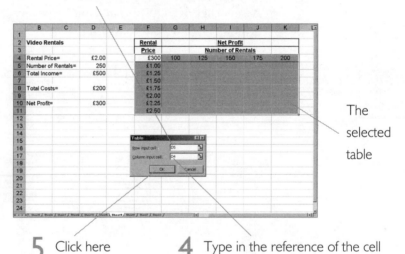

The selected table

Re step 4 – in the current example, the cell which relates to the rental price is D4.

5 Click here

4 Type in the reference of the cell which relates to the rental price

The table shows at a glance the rental price/ number of rentals relationship.

Rental		Net Profit			
Price		Number of Rentals			
£300	100	125	150	175	200
£1.00	-£100.00	-£75.00	-£50.00	-£25.00	£0.00
£1.25	-£75.00	-£43.75	-£12.50	£18.75	£50.00
£1.50	-£50.00	-£12.50	£25.00	£62.50	£100.00
£1.75	-£25.00	£18.75	£62.50	£106.25	£150.00
£2.00	£0.00	£50.00	£100.00	£150.00	£200.00
£2.25	£25.00	£81.25	£137.50	£193.75	£250.00
£2.50	£50.00	£112.50	£175.00	£237.50	£300.00

The completed table

What-If scenarios

Refer back to the illustration on page 112 and consider this:

Let's suppose we need to forecast the effect of changing the following values:

- the Rental Price (D4)

- the Number of Rentals (D5)

- the Total Costs (D8)

We could simply input revised values into the worksheet and observe the effect. However, if the revisions are simply putative, or if we need to input them more than once (or in varying combinations), it's best to use a scenario.

A scenario is simply a set of values you use to forecast the outcome of a worksheet model. You can:

- create new scenarios

- switch to and view existing scenarios

- return to the original worksheet values by invoking Undo

Creating a What-If scenario

Pull down the Tools menu and click Scenarios

You can create scenario summary reports. Click the Summary button in the Scenario Manager dialog. Follow the on-screen instructions.

To amend values in an existing scenario, select it in the Scenario Manager dialog. Click the Edit button. Now complete the Edit Scenario and Scenario Values dialogs in line with steps 3-7 overleaf. Finally, perform step 8.

To view a scenario in action, select it here:
Click the Show button. Finally, click Close when you've finished viewing the results.

To revert to the data values which preceded a scenario, press Ctrl+Z immediately after viewing it.

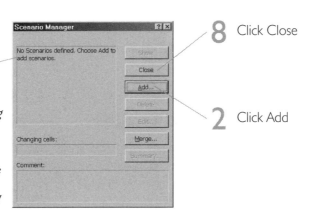

8 Click Close

2 Click Add

...cont'd

3 Name the scenario

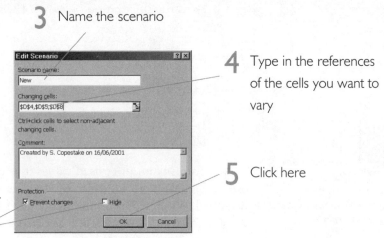

4 Type in the references of the cells you want to vary

5 Click here

To prevent anyone else amending your scenario, ensure Prevent changes is ticked. To hide it in the Scenario Manager dialog, tick Hide.

Re step 6 – at first, the existing values display; amend these as appropriate.

6 Type in What-if values

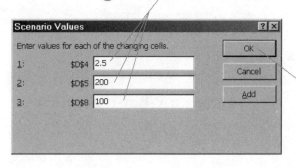

7 Click here then follow step 8 on page 119

Video Rentals	
Rental Price=	£2.50
Number of Rentals=	200
Total Income=	£500
Total Costs=	£100
Net Profit=	£400

The result of applying the scenario – see the HOT TIP on page 119

PivotTables

For more information on how to use lists, see chapter 11.

Another technique for reformulating information in a different way is the use of PivotTables. PivotTables provide much greater precision than any of the methods discussed earlier, and they function dynamically.

Using PivotTables

Re step 2 – you can also use external data sources (you may be prompted to install Microsoft Query). Click the relevant option and then complete the subsequent dialogs.

1 Click in the relevant list. Pull down the Data menu and click PivotTable and PivotChart Report

2 In the first dialog of the PivotTable and PivotChart Wizard, select 'Microsoft Excel list or database'. Ensure 'PivotTable' is selected, then click Next

3 In the second dialog, click Next

Re step 4 – click New worksheet or Existing worksheet. If the latter, enter the reference of the cell which will form the upper-left corner of the PivotTable.

4 In the third and final dialog, select where you want the PivotTable created. Click Finish. The wizard creates the PivotTable within Excel 2002 itself:

5 Drag any of the fields in the PivotTable Field List window to the appropriate PivotTable section...

PivotTables are particularly useful when you need to compare totals relating to detailed lists of figures. You can use PivotTable interactivity to resummarise data very conveniently.

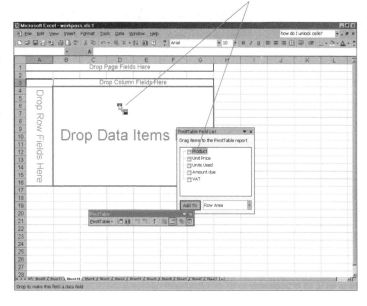

PivotTables are dynamic: you can drag any of the existing fields to new locations – or add new ones from the PivotTable Field List window. When you do so, Excel updates the PivotTable accordingly.

For access to Web PivotTables, enter 'PivotTable' into Excel's Ask-a-Question box and press Enter. In the list, click one of the Web-related entries.

You can create charts linked to PivotTable data. Click a cell in the PivotTable. Click this button:

in the Standard toolbar. The new PivotChart is dynamic:

You can add new fields at will...

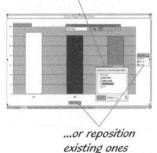

...or reposition existing ones

The end result:

The new PivotTable

	A	B	C	D	E
1					
2					
3	Sum of Amount due	Unit Price			
4	Units Used	£0.07	£0.08	£0.13	Grand Total
5	246			31.98	31.98
6	380		30.4		30.4
7	425	29.75			29.75
8	Grand Total	29.75	30.4	31.98	92.13

Excel has inserted the relevant totals/ sub-totals

Here, three of the fields in the list shown on page 124 – 'Units Used' and 'Unit Price' – have been associated with 'Amount Due'.

Using PivotTable AutoFormat

You can reformat PivotTables by applying AutoFormats (combinations of formatting characteristics). You can choose from more than 20.

Click in the PivotTable. Pull down the Format menu and select AutoFormat. Now do the following:

Click an AutoFormat

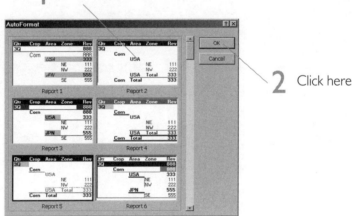

2 Click here

Using lists

You'll almost certainly want to use worksheets to store data in lists. Luckily, Excel 2002 lets you manage lists so that they return the data you want to view at any given time.

This chapter shows you how to create lists/databases. Once created, lists can be sorted in various ways to make your data more accessible. You can also filter data, so that information you don't want to view is temporarily excluded.

Covers

Chapter Eleven

Lists – an overview

In Excel 2002, a list is a series of worksheet rows which contain associated data (e.g. customer or supplier details).

Additionally, lists can function as databases. When they do:

- • use only one list per worksheet
- • the first row in any list must label the relevant columns
- • ensure rows have similar values in each column
- • ensure column names are formatted differently from list data
- • ensure the list is surrounded by at least one blank row AND one blank column
- • don't insert blank rows/ columns within the list
- • don't use spaces at the start or end of list cells

- the list columns become fields

- the column labels act as field names

- each row in the list is a unique record

Column (field) names

Product	Unit Price	Units Used	Amount due	VAT
Electricity	£0.07	425	£29.75	£5.21
Gas	£0.13	246	£31.98	£5.60
Water	£0.08	380	£30.40	£5.32

A simple list

Working with lists

When you've created a list, you can rearrange the data in various ways (Excel 2002 calls this 'sorting'). This is a useful technique. You can sort data:

In ascending sorts, Excel sorts in a specific order (shown first to last):

- in ascending order

- in descending order

- based on the contents of as many as four columns

- based on the contents of rows

- • numbers (minus to positive)
- • alphanumeric (left to right and character by character – apostrophes and commas are ignored)
- • logical values (FALSE precedes TRUE)
- • error values
- • blank cells

The order is reversed for descending sorts (except that blank cells are still last).

Other operations you can carry out on lists/databases include:

- inserting records via data forms

- applying simple filters with the use of AutoFilter

- applying complex filters with the use of criteria

To make sorting as effective as possible, lists should have column labels.

List sorting

You can also sort list rows by 2-3 columns. Perform steps 3–5 (in 3, select Sort top to bottom). Carry out steps 1–2; repeat them in respect of the 'Then by' fields lower down in the dialog, as appropriate. Finally, follow step 6.

(To sort by four columns, first click a cell in the list. Choose Data, Sort. In the Sort by box, select the least important column and click OK. Relaunch the Sort dialog. Select the most important column in the Sort by field, and the other two columns – in order of importance – in the Then by fields. Click OK.)

You can use a data form (a special dialog) to add a new record (row) to a list/database.

Click in the list. Pull down the Data menu and click Form. In the form, click New. Enter data for the new record, then press Enter. Repeat this process for as many records as you want to add. Finally, click Close.

When numbers are wrongly formatted as text in lists, Excel sorts detect this and treat the 'text' as numbers.

To carry out a sort, click any cell in the relevant list. Pull down the Data menu and click Sort. Then do one of the following:

- to perform a simple sort in ascending or descending order, carry out steps 1–2

- to sort list columns based on row contents, perform steps 3–5 first, then follow steps 1–2 (also complete the 'Then by' fields lower down the dialog, as appropriate)

(See also the HOT TIP.)

Finally, carry out step 6:

1 Click here; select the column you want to sort by

2 Select a sort order

6 Click here

3 Click here

5 Click here

4 Select Sort left to right (this sorts by rows – Sort top to bottom sorts by columns)

Using AutoFilter

You can use a special Excel 2002 feature – AutoFilter – to display only those list/database rows (records) which contain specific data.

Applying AutoFilter

Click a cell in the relevant list. Pull down the Data menu and click Filter, AutoFilter. Do the following:

In the column you want to filter, click here

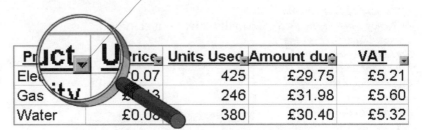

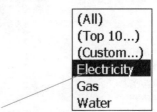

| (All) |
| (Top 10...) |
| (Custom...) |
| **Electricity** |
| Gas |
| Water |

2 Click the value you want to display

The end result

This is the result of applying the above AutoFilter:

Product	Unit Price	Units Used	Amount due	VAT
Electricity	£0.07	425	£29.75	£5.21

Applying criteria

The example used here is an instance of one condition applied over more than one column. You can also use several conditions in one column. For example, the following criteria range:

Country
England
France
Netherlands

displays those rows which contain 'England', 'France' or 'Netherlands' in the 'Country' column.

Filters created by AutoFilter are relatively limited – for instance, you can (in effect) only create and view matches with the use of the = comparison operator. You can't use any of Excel 2002's additional operators. (See page 44 for full details of comparison operators.)

You can, however, apply more complex filters with the use of criteria.

Applying criteria

Do the following:

1 Ensure your worksheet has a minimum of three blank rows (or preferably more) over the list you want to filter – the blank rows are known as the 'criteria range'

2 In the list, select the column labels which relate to the values you want to specify as filters. Press Ctrl+C

3 Click in the first blank row of your criteria range. Press Shift+Insert to insert the criteria labels

4 Type in the relevant criteria in the row immediately below the criteria labels:

In the criteria range on the right, all of the following criteria must be true for rows to display:

- *the 'Product' must be 'Gas'*
- *the 'Unit Price' must be greater than '£0.09'*
- *fewer than 400 units must have been used*

Criteria labels

Product	Unit Price	Units Used		
Gas	>£0.09	<400		
Product	**Unit Price**	**Units Used**	**Amount due**	**VAT**
Electricity	£0.07	425	£29.75	£5.21
Gas	£0.13	246	£31.98	£5.60
Water	£0.08	380	£30.40	£5.32

The criteria range

Perform the additional steps on page 128.

Now do the following:

5 Click anywhere in the list

6 Pull down the Data menu and click Filter, Advanced Filter

To apply the relevant filter in a different location, click here:

In the Copy to: field, type in the reference of the cell you want to form the upper-left corner of where you want the filtered rows inserted.

Finally, perform step 8.

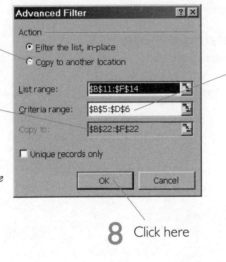

Advanced Filter

Action
- ⦿ Filter the list, in-place
- ○ Copy to another location

List range: `$B$11:$F$14`

Criteria range: `$B$5:$D$6`

Copy to: `$B$22:$F$22`

☐ Unique records only

OK   Cancel

7 Type in the criteria range reference (e.g. B5:D6)

Re step 7 – the criteria range must include the criteria labels to be effective.

8 Click here

The end result

This is the result of applying the advanced filter detailed on page 127:

Product	Unit Price	Units Used		
Gas	>£0.09	<400		
Product	**Unit Price**	**Units Used**	**Amount due**	**VAT**
Gas	£0.13	246	£31.98	£5.60

To remove a filter from a list, pull down the Data menu and click Show All.

Rows which don't match the criteria have been excluded

Multiple worksheets/workbooks

In this chapter, you'll learn how to create new worksheet windows and then rearrange them to best effect. You'll then set up/update data links between worksheets and workbooks, and create 3D references in formulas. Next, you'll discover how to achieve a useful overview by hiding rows and columns, then go on to apply manual and automatic outlining (together with styles) to lists. You'll also remove outlines.

Finally, you'll split worksheets into separate panes (so each can be viewed separately); freeze them for independent scrolling; and combine the two for best effect.

Covers

Chapter Twelve

Viewing several worksheets

Excel 2002 lets you view multiple worksheets simultaneously. This can be particularly useful when they have data in common. Viewing multiple worksheets is a two-stage process:

1. opening a new window

2. selecting the additional worksheet

Opening a new window

To switch between active windows, pull down the Window menu and click the relevant entry in the list at the bottom.

(Alternatively, click the relevant icon in the Windows Taskbar.)

Pull down the Window menu and do the following:

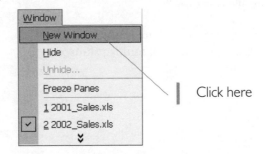

Click here

Selecting the additional worksheet

Excel now launches a new window showing an alternative view of the active worksheet. Do the following:

If you want to work with alternative views of the same worksheet – a useful technique in itself – simply omit step 2.

2 Click the relevant sheet tab

Rearranging worksheet windows

When you have multiple worksheet windows open at once, you can arrange them in specific patterns. This is a useful technique because it makes worksheets more visible and accessible. The available options are:

Use standard Windows techniques to move, close and resize open windows.

Tiled

Windows are displayed side by side:

Horizontal

Windows are displayed in a tiled column, with horizontal subdivisions:

Vertical

Windows are displayed in a tiled row, with vertical subdivisions:

Cascade

Windows are overlaid with a slight offset:

Rearranging windows

Pull down the Window menu and click Arrange. Do the following:

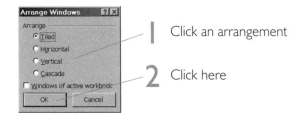

1 Click an arrangement

2 Click here

Links within a single workbook

Excel sometimes calls workbook links 'external references', and links to other programs 'remote references'.

Consider the following examples:

	A	B	C	D	E
1		**Sales Figures 2001**			
2		Qtr1	Qtr2	Qtr3	Qtr4
3		£9,000.00	£11,000.00	£17,000.00	£13,000.00

	A	B	C	D	E
1		**Sales Figures 2002**			
2		Qtr1	Qtr2	Qtr3	Qtr4
3		£10,000.00	£12,000.00	£19,000.00	£14,000.00

You can also set up links between separate workbooks – see page 134.

Here, we have extracts from two separate worksheets within the same workbook. The first records sales figures for 2001, the second sales figures for 2002. In the excerpts shown, the amount of data is small; there is really no reason why both sets of data shouldn't have been recorded on a single worksheet. However, where you're concerned with large amounts of data, it *is* a very good idea to record them on separate worksheets. By the same token, if you needed to record and collate the totals it would be advantageous to do this on a third worksheet…

In a link, if the name of another worksheet or workbook has characters which aren't alphabetic, it must be enclosed in single quotes.

Using lots of smaller worksheets (as opposed to a single, much larger sheet) produces the following benefits:

- your worksheets will recalculate faster (because large worksheets are much more unwieldy)

- it's much easier to remain in control of your worksheets

To remove the prompt from automatic updating (see the tips on the facing page), choose Tools, Options. Select the Edit tab. Untick Ask to update automatic links. Click OK. Now links are updated automatically at file startup, with no user involvement.

When you do use separate worksheets, you can 'link' the relevant data. To revert to the earlier example, the totals in the third worksheet could be linked to the relevant data in the 2001 Sales and 2002 Sales worksheets. This ensures that, when the contents of any of the relevant cells on the latter worksheets are changed, the totals are automatically updated.

...cont'd

When you create a link, the 'source' file holds the original information while the 'destination' file shows a copy of the data (because it retains only the address of the source file). As a result, the source file must always be accessible.

When you amend the source file while the destination file is active, the link in the destination file is automatically updated. Updating also occurs:

• *(the usual method) every time you open the destination file:*

Choose whether to update or not

• *when you perform a manual update. Choose Edit, Links. In the Edit Links dialog, select the relevant link(s) and click Update Values. Click OK*

Establishing links

Create the necessary additional worksheet. Then do the following:

This sheet refers to the illustrations on the facing page

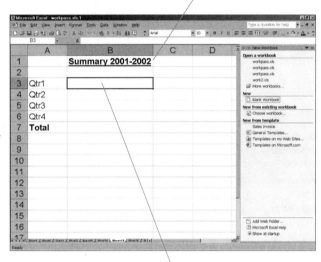

Select the cell you want to link

Now type in the required formula. Follow these rules:

1.   Type =

2.   Type in the reference to the cell on the first worksheet

3.   Type in the relevant operator – in this case, +

4.   Type in the reference to the cell on the second worksheet

5.   Press Enter

In our specific example (and given that the 2001 totals are on Sheet11 and the 2002 totals on Sheet12), the formula will be:

=Sheet11!B3+Sheet12!B3

Links between workbooks

To locate links, close all source files then carry out a search for square brackets – [ ] – since these are used to enclose the name of the source file.

See chapter 13 for more information on search operations.

You can also insert links to other workbooks, either open or on disk. Look at the illustration below:

	A	B
1		
2	2000	=SUM('C:\My Documents\[2000_Sales.xls]Sheet11'!B3)
3	2001	=SUM([2001_Sales.xls]Sheet12!B3)
4	2002	=Sheet2!B4
5		
6	Three Year Total	=SUM(B2:B4)

This is an excerpt from a new workbook: 2002_Sales.xls. This, as its name implies, totals sales for the years 2000-2002 inclusive. The formula in B2 is:

=SUM('C:\My Documents\[2000_Sales.xls]Sheet11'!B3)

Here, we're instructing Excel 2002 to refer to a workbook called 2000_Sales.xls in the My Documents folder. This workbook isn't currently open. Notice that:

You can have cell references in formulas include worksheet names by separating the name and reference with '!' (but omit the quote marks).

For example, to refer to cell 'A18' in worksheet '12', type:

Sheet12!A18

within the formula.

- the full workbook/worksheet address is enclosed in single quotes

- the workbook title is surrounded by square brackets

Study the formula for B3 below:

=SUM([2001_Sales.xls]Sheet12!B3)

Here, we don't need to specify the workbook address (i.e. the drive and folder) because the file is already open. Apart from this, however, the same syntax applies.

Use the syntax in the examples given here in your own linking formulas.

And the formula for B4:

=Sheet2!B4

This formula refers to a specific worksheet and cell within the current workbook (2002_Sales.xls) using the standard techniques we've discussed in earlier chapters.

3D references

In the example discussed on pages 132 and 133, all the worksheets have exactly the same format in that each quarterly amount lies in the same cell on each sheet. When this is the case, you can use an alternative method of summarising the sales figures on the third sheet: 3D referencing. Using 3D references is often quicker and more convenient.

3D references consist of both of the following:

• a sheet range (i.e. the beginning and end sheets are specified, separated by a colon)

• a standard cell range

Entering a 3D reference

Not all Excel 2002 functions support 3D referencing. Those that do include:

• *Average*

• *Count*

• *Max*

• *Min*

• *Sum*

Select the relevant cell. Type in the required formula. As you do so, follow these rules:

1. Type =

2. Type in the appropriate function (see the BEWARE tip), then (

3. Type in the reference to the first worksheet, followed by a colon

4. Type in the reference to the final worksheet

5. Type !

6. Type in the cell range in the normal way, then)

7. Press Enter

You can't use the intersection operator in 3D referencing.

In our specific example (and given that the 2001 totals are on Sheet11 and the 2002 totals on Sheet12, both in cell B3), the 3D formula will be:

=Sum(Sheet11:Sheet12!B3)

Hiding data

If a worksheet contains a mass of information, you can temporarily hide some of the data to get an overview.

Hiding rows and columns

Select the row(s) or column(s) to be hidden. Pull down the Format menu and select Row, Hide or Column, Hide

An example – here, rows 5 and 6 have been hidden

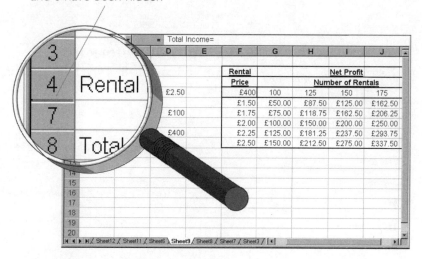

Unhiding rows and columns

Make a selection which includes the row(s) or column(s). (For instance, to unhide rows 5 and 6 in the example above, select rows 4–7 inclusive). Pull down the Format menu and click Row, Unhide or Column, Unhide

Outlining

Outlines use levels (up to 8) to allow you to expand or collapse sections of a worksheet at will, and are nested (each inner level supplies details of the earlier outer one).

An alternative way to hide rows or columns temporarily is to outline (or group) them. When you apply outlining to specific data within a worksheet, Excel 2002 inserts an Outline Level Bar against it. You can then specify whether the data displays or not.

Applying outlining

You can only apply outlining to lists. (For more on lists, see Chapter 11.)

1. Select one or more rows or columns containing the data you want to outline

2. Pull down the Data menu and click Group and Outline, Group

The end result

In the example below, rows 3–6 have been outlined, and will be hidden (see page 138):

Before you create an outline, ensure that the relevant rows are together. Also, make sure summary rows are present above or below each group of detail rows.

Outline Level bars – see page 138 for how to use them

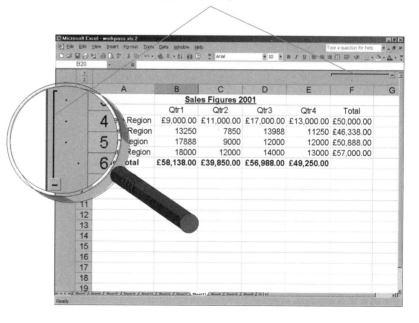

To hide the Outline Level bar(s), pull down the Tools menu and click Options. Activate the View tab and deselect Outline symbols. Click OK.

Here, the range F3:F6 has also been grouped.

In outlinable lists, summary rows (i.e. those which contain totals) must be below the list data, while summary columns must be to the right.

You can apply automatic styles to outlines. First, select the relevant cells. Pull down the Data menu and click Group and Outline, Settings. Tick Automatic styles then click Apply styles.

You can also hide or unhide data levels by referring to the row or column level symbols below the Name box. Do the following:

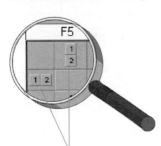

Click the smaller number(s) to hide data, the larger numbers to reveal it

Hiding outlined data

To hide data which you've outlined, do the following:

Click here

Unhiding outlined data

To unhide data which you've outlined, do the following:

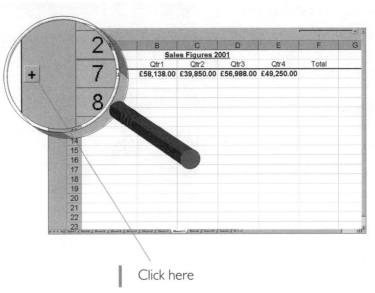

Click here

In this example, attempting to select rows 2–7 en masse produces an error message:

Click OK

Instead, the cells which relate to the hidden rows have been selected.

You can have Excel apply an automatic outline in the following situation:

- *when summary formulas (e.g. SUM) refer to the detail data*
- *when all the columns with summary formulas are to the left or right of detail data*

First select the relevant cells. Pull down the Data menu and click Group and Outline, Auto Outline.

If you pre-select one or more whole rows or columns rather than a cell range (as here), Excel 2002 may not launch the Ungroup dialog.

Removing outlines

If you want to remove an outline, make a selection which includes the appropriate row(s) or column(s). In the illustration below, rows 3–6 have previously been outlined and are currently hidden; to remove this outlining, cells A2:E7 have been selected (see the DON'T FORGET tip):

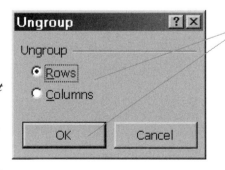

| | Pull down the Data menu and click Group and Outline, Ungroup |

2 Make the relevant selection and confirm

Splitting worksheets

Excel 2002 has two further techniques you can use to make complex worksheets easier to understand. You can:

- split worksheets horizontally or vertically into panes

- freeze individual panes, so that the data they contain doesn't scroll

Splitting worksheets

In the example shown here, a single cell in column D was selected before step 1 was performed; as a result, Excel has inserted two Split bars and created four panes.

(Pre-selecting a row or column results in one Split bar and two panes being inserted.)

1 Select the row or column before which you want the worksheet to be split, or simply select one cell for a double split (as below)

2 Pull down the Window menu and click Split

With purely horizontal splits, dragging either scroll box on the right of the screen moves the respective pane (but not the other) up or down. Dragging the horizontal scroll box, however, moves both panes to the right or left.

With vertical splits, the vertical scroll box moves both panes, while the horizontal scroll boxes are pane-specific.

Double-splits, as here, combine both aspects.

Four panes

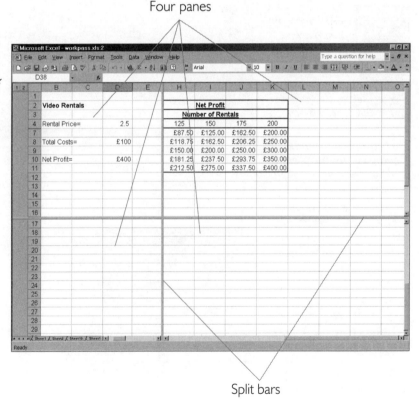

Split bars

Freezing worksheets

Perform ONE of A., B. or C. (as appropriate) then carry out step 1:

A.   To create two panes with the top pane frozen, select the row above which you want the split inserted

B.   To create two panes with the left pane frozen, select the column to the left of which you want the split inserted

C.   To create four panes with the upper and left panes frozen, select the cell to the right of, and below, where you want the split inserted

| Pull down the Window menu and click Freeze

Create the precise effect you need by using split and freeze combinations.

Here, column E was selected before the worksheet was frozen, thereby creating a vertical freeze.
Dragging the horizontal scroll bar moves only the right-hand pane to the left or right but has no effect on the left-hand pane. On the other hand, the effect of dragging the vertical scroll bar is unchanged (both panes move up or down).
This situation is reversed for horizontal freezes.

A vertical
Freeze split

	B	C	D	E	F	G	H	I	J	K	L
1											
2	Video Rentals				Rental		Net Profit				
3					Price		Number of Rentals				
4	Rental Price=		2.5		£400	100	125	150	175	200	
7					£1.50	£50.00	£87.50	£125.00	£162.50	£200.00	
8	Total Costs=		£100		£1.75	£75.00	£118.75	£162.50	£206.25	£250.00	
9					£2.00	£100.00	£150.00	£200.00	£250.00	£300.00	
10	Net Profit=		£400		£2.25	£125.00	£181.25	£237.50	£293.75	£350.00	
11					£2.50	£150.00	£212.50	£275.00	£337.50	£400.00	
12											
13											
14											
15											
16											
17											
18											
19											
20											
21											
22											
23											
24											
25											
26											

Sheet1 / Sheet8 / Sheet10 / Sheet14 / Sheet13 / Sheet12 / Sheet17 / Sheet11 / Sheet6 / Sheet16 \ Sheet9

Adjusting worksheet splits

Redefining a split

You can adjust a split with the use of the mouse. Move the mouse pointer over the Split Bar – it changes to: ⬥ or ⬌

Re step 1 – you can't use this technique with frozen worksheets.

Now carry out the following:

Drag the Split Bar to a new location

Split actions can't be undone.

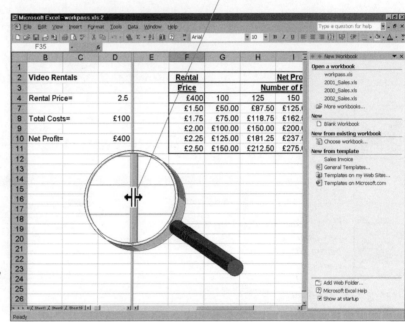

You can't remove splits in frozen worksheets by double-clicking them.

Instead, pull down the Window menu and click Remove Split (this also unfreezes the relevant panes).

Removing a split

Double-click the Split bar

Unfreezing a worksheet

Pull down the Window menu and click Unfreeze Panes

Formatting worksheets

In this chapter, you'll learn to customise cell formatting. You'll specify how cell contents align (including text), apply fonts and type sizes and border cells (including dynamically with the Border pencil). You'll also fill cells; format data automatically; and transfer formatting between cells. Then you'll use conditional formatting to have Excel flag cells which meet specific criteria. Finally, you'll carry out data searches/substitutions and create/apply styles to make formatting even easier.

Covers

Chapter Thirteen

Cell alignment

Note that the main horizontal alignment types are:

General — *the default (see the first paragraph on the right)*

Left — *the contents are aligned from the left*

Center — *the contents are centred*

Right — *the contents are aligned from the right*

Fill — *the contents are duplicated so that they fill the cell*

Justify — *a combination of Left and Right*

By default, Excel aligns text to the left of cells, and numbers to the right. However, you can change this. Alignments come under two basic headings: horizontal and vertical.

You can also amend rotation (the direction of text flow within cells) by specifying a plus (anticlockwise) or minus (clockwise) angle. And you can apply text wrap – this forces any surplus text onto separate lines within the host cell (instead of overflowing into adjacent cells to the right).

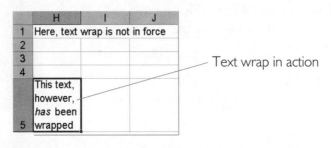

Text wrap in action

Customising cell alignment

Select the cell(s) whose contents you want to realign. Pull down the Format menu and click Cells. Carry out step 1 below. Follow steps 2-4, as appropriate, then finally step 5.

Note that the vertical alignment types are:

Top — *cell contents align with the top of the cell(s)*

Center — *the contents are centred*

Bottom — *the contents align with the cell bottom*

Justify — *the contents are aligned along the top and bottom of the cell(s)*

1 Ensure the Alignment tab is active

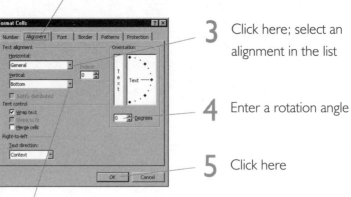

3 Click here; select an alignment in the list

4 Enter a rotation angle

5 Click here

2 Click here; select an alignment in the list

Changing fonts and styles

Don't confuse font styles with overall styles (collections of formatting aspects).

See pages 154–158 for how to use overall styles.

Excel lets you carry out the following actions on cell contents (numbers and/or text). You can:

- apply a new font and/or type size

- apply a font style (for most fonts, you can choose from: Regular, Italic, Bold or Bold Italic)

- apply a colour

- apply a special effect: <u>underlining</u>, ~~strikethrough~~, superscript or subscript

Amending the appearance of cell contents

Select the cell(s) whose contents you want to reformat. Pull down the Format menu and click Cells. Carry out step 1 below. Now follow any of steps 2-5, as appropriate, or either or both of the HOT TIPS. Finally, carry out step 6.

To underline the specified contents, click the arrow to the right of the Underline box; select an underlining type in the list.

1 Ensure the Font tab is active

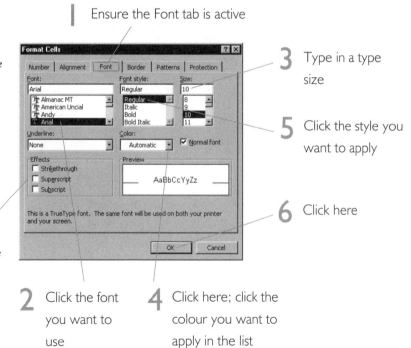

3 Type in a type size

5 Click the style you want to apply

6 Click here

To apply a special effect, click any of the options in the Effects section.

2 Click the font you want to use

4 Click here; click the colour you want to apply in the list

Bordering cells

Excel 2002 lets you define a border around:

- the perimeter of a selected cell range

- specific sides within a cell range

You can customise the border by choosing from a selection of pre-defined border styles. You can also add new line styles to specific sides, or colour the border.

Applying a cell border – the dialog route

First, select the cell range you want to border. Pull down the Format menu and click Cells. Now carry out step 1 below. Follow step 2 to apply an overall border. Carry out step 3 if you want to deactivate one or more border sides. Perform step 4 if you want to colour the border. Finally, carry out step 5:

If you want to customise the border style, click a line style here:
immediately after step 2. Omit step 3. Follow step 4 if you want to colour the new style. Now do the following in this part of the dialog:

Click any of the 4 borders to apply the new style

Finally, carry out step 5.

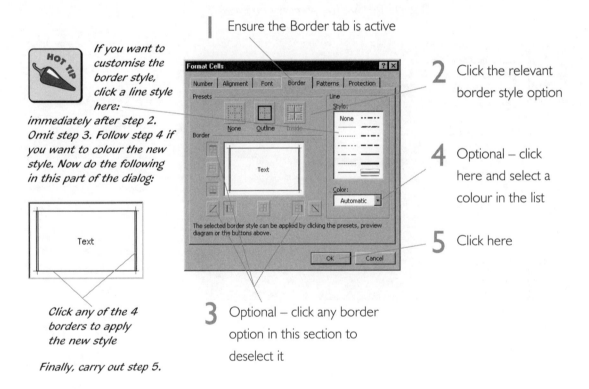

Ensure the Border tab is active

2 Click the relevant border style option

4 Optional – click here and select a colour in the list

5 Click here

3 Optional – click any border option in this section to deselect it

Applying a cell border – the Pencil route

 In the Formatting toolbar (or its fly-out), click here:

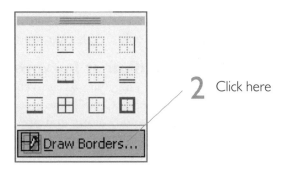

2 Click here

5 Ensure this is selected

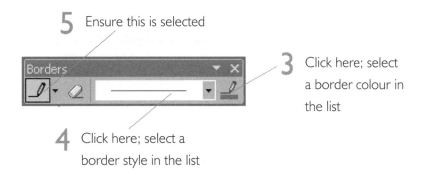

3 Click here; select a border colour in the list

4 Click here; select a border style in the list

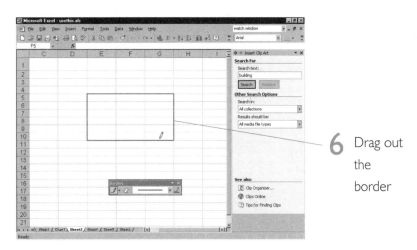

6 Drag out the border

Shading cells

Excel 2002 lets you apply the following to cells:

- a background colour

- a foreground pattern

- a foreground colour

Interesting effects can be achieved by using pattern and colour combinations with coloured backgrounds.

Applying a pattern or background

First, select the cell range you want to shade. Pull down the Format menu and click Cells. Now carry out step 1. Perform step 2 to apply a *background* colour, and/or 3-5 to apply a *foreground* pattern or a pattern/colour combination. Finally, follow step 6.

1 Ensure the Patterns tab is active

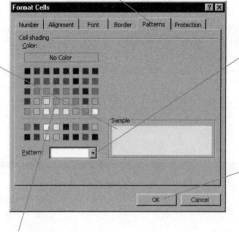

3 Click here to apply a foreground pattern or a pattern/colour combination

6 Click here

2 Click a colour here to apply it as a background

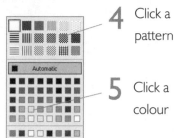

4 Click a pattern

5 Click a colour

AutoFormat

Excel 2002 provides a shortcut to the formatting of worksheet data: AutoFormat.

AutoFormat consists of 16 pre-defined formatting schemes. These incorporate specific excerpts from the font, number, alignment, border and shading options discussed earlier. You can apply any of these schemes (and their associated formatting) to selected cell ranges with just a few mouse clicks. You can even specify which scheme elements you *don't* wish to use.

AutoFormat works with most arrangements of worksheet data.

Using AutoFormat

First, select the cell range you want to apply an automatic format to. Pull down the Format menu and click AutoFormat. Now carry out step 1 below. Steps 2-3 are optional. Finally, follow step 4:

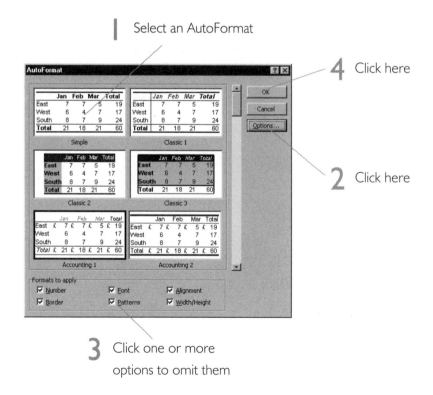

1 Select an AutoFormat

4 Click here

2 Click here

3 Click one or more options to omit them

The Format Painter

Excel 2002 provides a very useful tool which can save you a lot of time and effort: the Format Painter. You can use the Format Painter to copy the formatting attributes from cells you've previously formatted to other cells, in one operation.

Using the Format Painter

1 Apply the necessary formatting, if you haven't already done so. Then select the formatted cells

2 Click the Format Painter icon in the Standard toolbar (or its fly-out)

Re. step 2 – double-click the Format Painter icon if you want to apply the selected formatting more than once. Then repeat step 3 as often as necessary. Press Esc when you've finished.

Pre-formatted text – see step 1

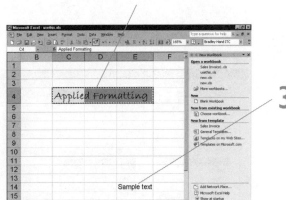

3 Select the cell(s) you want the formatting copied to

When you've finished using the Format Painter (or before, if you decide you don't want to proceed), press Esc.

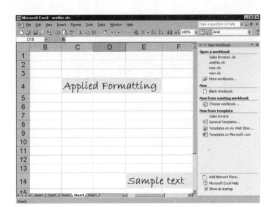

The end result

Conditional formatting

Formatting which alters cell size (e.g. font changes) can't be used as a conditional format. As a result, these options are greyed out in the Format Cells dialog.

You can have Excel 2002 apply conditional formats to specific cells. Conditional formats are formatting attributes (e.g. colour or shading) which Excel imposes on cells when the criteria you set are met. Conditional formats help you identify cells and monitor worksheets.

For instance, in a worksheet in which B10 is the total of the number of videos rented out, you could tell Excel 2002 to colour B10 in red if the value it contains falls below a certain level, or in blue if it exceeds it...

Applying conditional formatting

To add more than 1 condition, click Add then repeat steps 1-6.

Select the relevant cell(s). Pull down the Format menu and click Conditional Formatting. Now do the following:

1 Click here; select a comparison phrase

2 Type in 1 or more match values

If you want, you can use a TRUE/FALSE formula to define the match.
Click here:
Select Formula Is. Now type the formula in the field to the right. Finally, carry out steps 3–7, as appropriate.

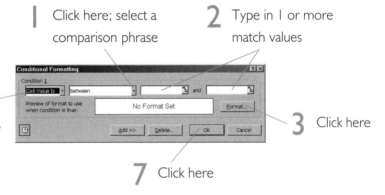

3 Click here

7 Click here

To find conditional formatting, press F5. Click Special. Select Conditional formats, then All to find any conditional formatting, or Same to find cells with the same conditional formatting. Click OK.

4 Activate a tab

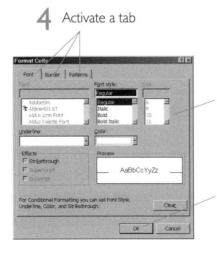

5 Select the appropriate formatting – the options depend on the tab chosen in step 4

6 Click here

Find operations

Excel 2002 lets you search for and jump to text or numbers (in short, any information) in your worksheets. This is a particularly useful feature when worksheets become large and complex.

You can organise your search by rows or by columns. You can also specify whether Excel looks in:

- cells that contain formulas

- cells that don't contain formulas

Additionally, you can insist that Excel only flag exact matches (i.e. if you searched for '11', Excel would not find '1111'), and you can also limit text searches to text which has the case you specified (e.g. searching for 'PRODUCT LIST' would not find 'Product List' or 'product list').

To search for data over more than one worksheet, select the relevant sheet tabs before launching the Find dialog.

If you want to restrict the search to specific cells, select a cell range before you launch the Find and Replace dialog.

Searching for data

Place the mouse pointer at the location in the active worksheet from which you want the search to begin. Pull down the Edit menu and click Find. Now carry out step 1 below, then (optionally) 2. Finally, carry out step 3.

1 Type in the data you want to find

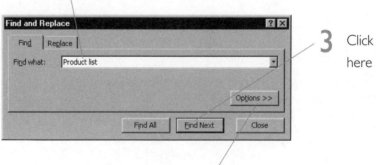

3 Click here

2 To specify the search direction, limit it to certain cell types or make it case-specific, click Options and complete the dialog which appears

Find-and-replace operations

When you search for data, you can also – if you want – have Excel 2002 replace it with something else.

Find-and-replace operations can be organised by rows or columns. However, unlike straight searches, you can't specify whether Excel looks in cells that contain formulas or not. As with straight searches, you can, however, limit find-and-replace operations to exact matches and also (in the case of text) to precise case matches.

Normally, find-and-replace operations only affect the host worksheet. If you want to carry out an operation over multiple worksheets, see the HOT TIP.

Running a find-and-replace operation

Place the mouse pointer at the location in the active worksheet from which you want the search to begin (or select a cell range if you want to restrict the find-and-replace operation to this). Pull down the Edit menu and click Replace. Now carry out steps 1-4 below. Finally, carry out step 5 as often as required, or perform step 6 once for a global substitution.

To replace data over more than one worksheet, select the relevant sheet tabs before launching the Find and Replace dialog.

If, when you carry out step 5, Excel finds an instance of the search text you don't want replaced, simply repeat step 4 instead.

1 Type in the data you want to find

2 Type in replacement data

3 To set options (see step 2 on the facing page) click here

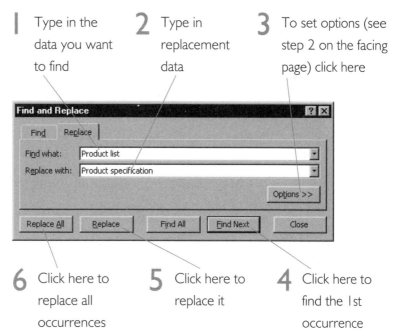

6 Click here to replace all occurrences

5 Click here to replace it

4 Click here to find the 1st occurrence

Styles – an overview

Styles are named collections of associated formatting commands.

The advantage of using styles is that you can apply more than one formatting enhancement to selected cells in one go. Once a style is in place, you can change one or more elements of it and have Excel 2002 apply the amendments automatically throughout the whole of the active workbook.

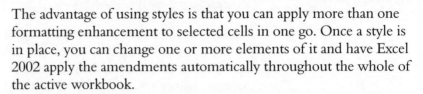

For how to apply outline styles, see chapter 12.

Generally, new workbooks you create in Excel 2002 have the following pre-defined styles as a minimum:

Comma	Only includes numeric formatting – numerals are shown with two decimal places
Comma (0)	Only includes numeric formatting – numerals are shown with 0 decimal places
Currency	Only includes numeric formatting – numerals are shown with two decimal places and the default currency symbol
Currency (0)	Only includes numeric formatting – numerals are shown with 0 decimal places and the default currency symbol
Normal	The default. Includes numeric, alignment, font and border/shading formatting – numerals are shown with 0 decimal places
Percent	Only includes numeric formatting – data is expressed as a percentage

You can easily create (and apply) your own styles.

Creating a style

The easiest way to create a style is to:

A. apply the appropriate formatting enhancements to one or more specific cells and then select them

B. tell Excel 2002 to create a new style based on this formatting

First, carry out A. above. Then pull down the Format menu and do the following:

Keep styles simple. Select only single cells or cells with identical formatting.

(Styles are not suitable for ranges of cells with different outline borders.)

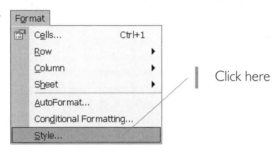

Click here

If you're used to using styles in Word 2002, you'll find Excel's styles simple to use.

2 Type in the new style's name

When you've finished using the Style dialog, click Close.

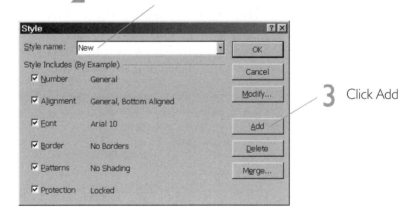

3 Click Add

See page 156 for how to use your new style.

Applying styles

Excel 2002 makes applying styles easy.

First, select the cell(s) you want to apply the style to. Pull down the Format menu and click Style. Now do the following:

Click here; in the list, click
the style you want to apply

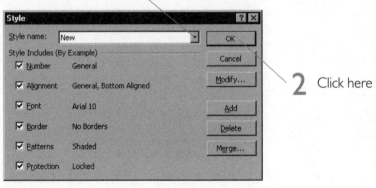

2 Click here

Shortcut for applying styles

Excel makes it even easier to apply styles if you currently have the Formatting toolbar on-screen. (If you haven't, pull down the View menu and click Toolbars, Formatting.)

Select the cell(s) you want to apply the style to. Then do the following:

The Style box

Click here

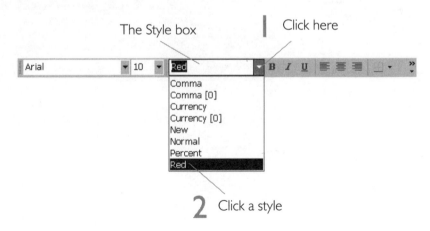

2 Click a style

Amending styles

The easiest way to modify an existing style is to:

A.   apply the appropriate formatting enhancements to one or more cells and then select them

B.   use the Style dialog to select a style and tell Excel to assign the selected formatting to it

1 First, carry out A. above. Then pull down the Format menu and click Style

Re step 2 – you must type in the name of the style you want to amend (clicking in the Style name field and selecting it in the list doesn't work).

2 Type in the name of the style you want to amend

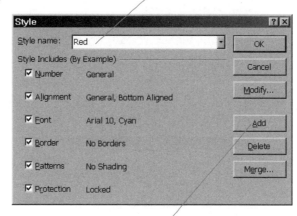

3 Click here

4 Click the Close button to apply the style change(s) to all examples of the style (but only in the current workbook)

Deleting and copying styles

Good housekeeping sometimes makes it necessary to remove unwanted styles from the active document. Excel 2002 lets you do this very easily.

Another useful feature is the ability to copy ('merge') styles from one workbook to another.

Deleting styles

1 Pull down the Format menu and click Style

2 In the Style dialog, select a style in the Style name field. Click Delete – deletion is immediate. Click OK

Copying styles

1 Open the workbook from which you want to copy styles, then the workbook you want to copy them into

2 Pull down the Format menu and click Style

A special situation occurs if the workbook you're copying from has styles with the same name as the target workbook. If this is so, Excel launches a special message after step 4:

Click Yes to overwrite the target file's styles

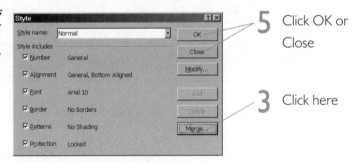

5 Click OK or Close

3 Click here

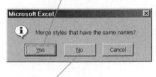

Or click No to retain the original style format

4 Double-click the workbook which contains the styles you want to copy – Excel now imports the styles

Printing worksheets

With the size of many worksheets, successful printing is an issue. Fortunately, Excel 2002 lets you customise printed output with a very high level of precision.

In this chapter, you'll learn how to prepare your worksheets for printing. This involves specifying the paper size/orientation, margins and page numbering; inserting headers/footers (you'll also create your own designs); 'autoscaling' output so it fits a given page width; using collation; and generally maximising your use of space on the printed page. Then you'll launch and use Print Preview mode (to proof your worksheets) and use Page Break Preview to customise the printable area on-the-fly. Finally, you'll specify which worksheet components should be printed (and how) and define Print areas via a dialog route.

Covers

Chapter Fourteen

Page setup – an overview

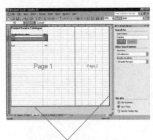

Drag page break margins to customise the printable area

(To leave Page Break Preview when you've finished with it, click Normal in the View menu.)

Making sure your worksheets print with the correct page setup can be a complex issue, for the simple reason that most worksheets become very extensive with the passage of time (so large, in fact, that in the normal course of things they won't fit onto a single page).

Page setup features you can customise include:

• the paper size and orientation

• scaling

• the starting page number

• the print quality

• margins

• header/footer information

• page order

• which worksheet components print

Margin settings you can amend are:

• top

• bottom

• left

• right

Additionally, you can set the distance between the top page edge and the top of the header, and the distance between the bottom page edge and the bottom edge of the footer.

When you save your active workbook, all Page Setup settings are saved with it.

Setting worksheet options

The Page Setup dialog for charts in chart sheets has a special tab – see chapter 15 for how to use this.

Excel 2002 lets you:

- define a printable area on-screen

- define a column or row title which will print on every page

- specify which worksheet components should print

- print with minimal formatting

- determine the print direction

If you want to restrict the print-run to a specific cell range ('print area'), enter the address in the Print area field.

(You can also do this in Page Break Preview. Select the relevant cells then pull down the File menu and click Print Area, Set Print Area.)

Using the Sheet tab in the Page Setup dialog

Pull down the File menu and click Page Setup. Now carry out step 1 below, followed by steps 2-4 (and the tips) as appropriate. Finally, carry out step 5.

1 | Ensure the Sheet tab is active

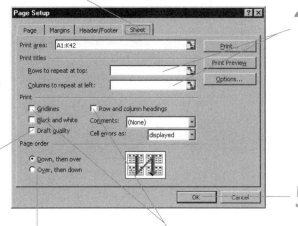

4 Type in the address of the row/column you want to use as a consistent title

Re step 3 – to speed up printing, ensure Gridlines isn't ticked.

Click Draft Quality for rapid printing with the minimum of formatting.

5 Click here

2 Click a direction option

3 Click a component to include or exclude it

Excel should automatically switch between the Letter and A4 page sizes, as and when necessary.

Setting page options

Excel 2002 comes with 15 pre-defined paper sizes which you can apply to your worksheets, in either portrait (top-to-bottom) or landscape (sideways on) orientation. This is one approach to effective printing. Another is scaling: you can print out your worksheets as they are, or you can have Excel shrink them so that they fit a given paper size (you can even automate this process). Additionally, you can set the print resolution and starting page number.

Using the Page tab in the Page Setup dialog

Pull down the File menu and click Page Setup. Now carry out step 1 below, followed by steps 2-6 as appropriate. Finally, carry out step 7:

Re step 2 – Landscape orientation lets you fit in far more columns.

Re step 5 – by default, Excel numbers pages from '1'. Leave the First page number field setting as Auto if you want this.

To make your worksheet print in a specific number of pages, complete the 'Fit to' fields.

(Alternatively, enter '1' in the first field and leave the second blank to have Excel 'autoscale' the worksheet so that it fits the paper width.)

Re step 4 – reducing the scaling percentage is a way of getting more data on the page (but check the font size in Print Preview before printing).

1 Ensure the Page tab is active

2 Click the orientation you need

3 Click here; click the page size you need in the drop-down list

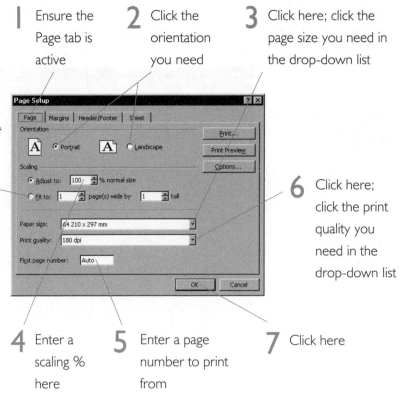

6 Click here; click the print quality you need in the drop-down list

4 Enter a scaling % here

5 Enter a page number to print from

7 Click here

Setting margin options

Excel inserts page breaks automatically. If you need to override these, click the row, column or cell where you want the new page to begin. Pull down the Insert menu and click Page Break.

To view automatic page breaks, pull down the Tools menu and click Options. Activate the View tab. Ensure Page breaks is selected. Click OK.

Excel 2002 lets you set a variety of margin settings. The illustration below shows the main ones:

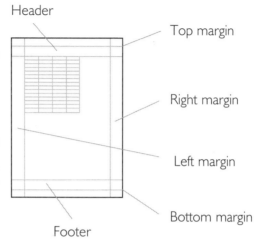

Header

Top margin

Right margin

Left margin

Bottom margin

Footer

Adjusting margin settings is one way to get more data on the page (another is to apply Landscape orientation – see the facing page).

Using the Margins tab in the Page Setup dialog

Pull down the File menu and click Page Setup. Now carry out step 1 below, followed by steps 2-3 as appropriate. Finally, carry out step 4:

1 Ensure the Margins tab is active

To specify how your worksheet aligns on the page, click either option here.

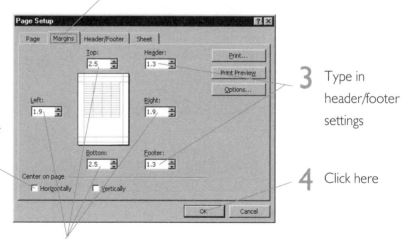

3 Type in header/footer settings

4 Click here

2 Type in the margin settings you need

Setting header/footer options

Excel 2002 provides a list of built-in header and footer settings. You can apply any of these to the active worksheet. These settings include:

Note that you can also use specific groups of header/ footer settings

e.g.:

• *Page 1, Book 1*

• *Confidential, Sheet 1, Page 1*

- the worksheet title

- the workbook title

- the page number

- the user's name

- 'Confidential'

- the date

Using the Header/Footer tab in the Page Setup dialog

Pull down the File menu and click Page Setup. Now carry out step 1 below, followed by steps 2-3 as appropriate. Finally, carry out step 4:

To set up your own header or footer, click Custom Header or Custom Footer. Complete the dialog which launches.

For example, enter text in the Left section, Center section and/or Right section fields and select it. Click the Font button in the dialog's toolbar and apply the relevant formatting... Or click in a section and select one of the other buttons to insert features such as the date, time or file path details. Alternatively, click this button:

to insert a picture (complete the Insert Picture dialog).

| Ensure the Header/ Footer tab is active

2 Click here; select a header from the list

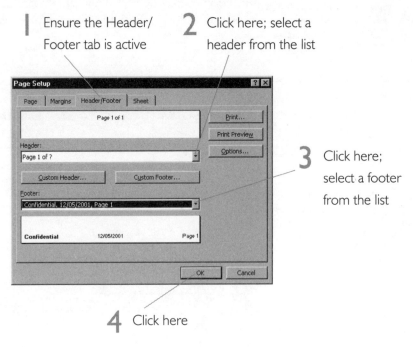

3 Click here; select a footer from the list

4 Click here

Launching Print Preview

Print Preview displays data in greyscale (rather than colour).

Excel 2002 provides a special view mode called Print Preview. This displays the active worksheet as it will look when printed. Use Print Preview as a final check just before you begin printing.

You can perform the following actions from within Print Preview:

*   moving from page to page

*   zooming in or out on the active page

Excel's Print Preview mode only has the following Zoom settings:

*   adjusting most Page Setup settings

*   adjusting margins visually

*   Full Page
*   High-Magnification

Launching Print Preview

Pull down the File menu and click Print Preview. This is the result:

Special Print Preview toolbar

To leave Print Preview mode and return to your worksheet (or chart sheet), simply press Esc.

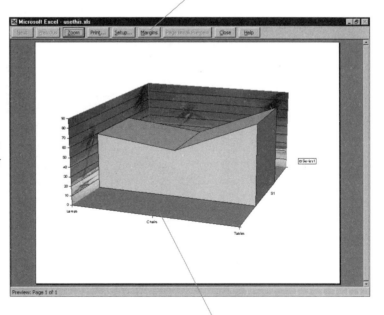

See Chapter 15 for how to work with charts.

A preview of a chart sheet

Working with Print Preview

All of the operations you can perform in Print Preview mode can be accessed via the toolbar.

Click the Page Break Preview button to launch Page Break Preview – see the HOT TIP on page 160 for how to use it.

Using the Print Preview toolbar

Do any of the following, as appropriate:

I Click Next to jump to the next page

3 Click here to zoom in or out

6 Click here to launch the Page Setup dialog

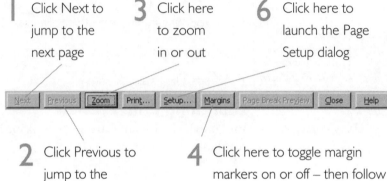

Re step 6 – see earlier topics (pages 160– 164) for how to use the Page Setup dialog.

2 Click Previous to jump to the previous page

4 Click here to toggle margin markers on or off – then follow step 5

5 Drag any margin to reposition it

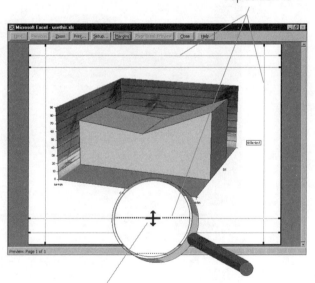

Magnified view of Move pointer

Printing worksheet data

Excel 2002 lets you specify:

- the number of copies you want printed

Collation is only enabled if you're printing more than one page.

- whether you want the copies 'collated'. This is the process whereby Excel prints one full copy at a time. For instance, if you're printing three copies of a 10-page worksheet, Excel prints pages 1-10 of the first copy, followed by pages 1-10 of the second and pages 1-10 of the third

- which pages (or page ranges) you want printed

- whether you want the print run restricted to cells you selected before initiating printing

You can 'mix and match' these, as appropriate.

To select and print more than one worksheet, hold down Shift as you click on multiple tabs in the worksheet Tab area.

Starting a print run

Open the workbook that contains the data you want to print. If you want to print an entire worksheet, click the relevant tab in the worksheet Tab area. If you need to print a specific cell range within a worksheet, select it. Then pull down the File menu and click Print. Do any of steps 1-5. Then carry out step 6 to begin printing.

Click here; select the printer you want from the list

To adjust your printer's internal settings before you initiate printing, click Properties... Then refer to your printer's manual.

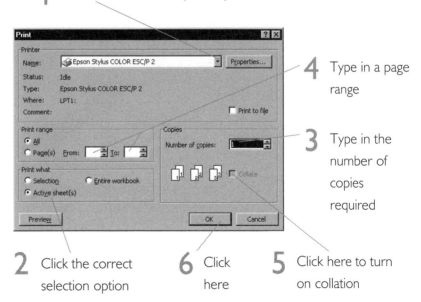

4 Type in a page range

3 Type in the number of copies required

2 Click the correct selection option

6 Click here

5 Click here to turn on collation

Printing – the fast-track approach

There are occasions when you'll merely want to print out your work:

- without having to invoke the Print dialog

- with the current settings applying

- with a single mouse click

One reason for doing this is proofing. Irrespective of how thoroughly you check documents on-screen, there will always be errors and deficiencies which, with the best will in the world, are difficult or impossible to pick up. By initiating printing with the minimum of delay, you can check your work that much more rapidly...

For this reason, Excel 2002 provides a printing method which is especially quick and easy to use.

Printing with the current print options

First, ensure your printer is ready and on-line. Make sure the Standard toolbar is visible. (If it isn't, pull down the View menu and click Toolbars, Standard). Now do the following:

Click here

Excel 2002 starts printing the active worksheet immediately, using the defaults listed above.

Charts and graphics

Charts and other graphic elements make your worksheets more attractive and make data more approachable.

In this chapter, you'll learn how to create and insert new charts (both as objects within worksheets and as separate chart sheets) in order to make your data more immediate and accessible, then go on to convert existing charts into another type. You'll save your charts to Web/FTP sites and intranets (both interactively and non-interactively) then customise chart-specific page setup issues. You'll insert pictures into your worksheets (including from the Web) and go on to manipulate them. Finally, you'll insert AutoShapes (extraordinarily flexible graphic shapes), reformat existing ones and add text to them.

All of these techniques dramatically improve worksheet impact.

Covers

Chapter Fifteen

Charting – an overview

Excel 2002 has comprehensive charting capabilities. You can have it convert selected data into its visual equivalent. This makes information much easier to follow and far more dramatic.

Excel offers a wide number of chart formats/sub-formats.

You can create a chart:

- as a picture within the parent worksheet

- as a separate chart sheet

Chart sheets have their own tabs in the Tab area; these operate just like worksheet tabs.

Excel uses a special Wizard – the Chart Wizard – to make the process of creating charts as easy and convenient as possible.

Charts are linked to the originating data – this means that, if you amend the data, the chart is updated automatically.

When you create a chart, column/row headings become axis or series names.

As here, you can add a picture to chart walls. See page 178.

When you resize a chart, fonts rescale automatically, for increased legibility.

You can make the edges of line charts less jagged. Select the relevant data series. Pull down the Format menu and choose Selected Data Series. Select the Patterns tab and tick Smoothed line. Click OK.

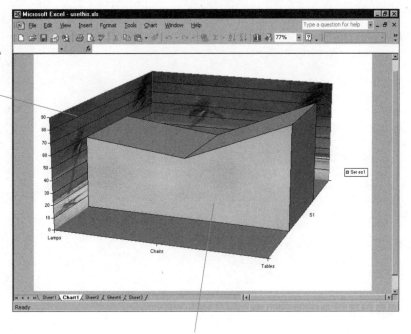

A 3-D Area chart

Creating a chart

First, select the cells you want converted into a chart. Pull down the Insert menu and click Chart. The first Chart Wizard dialog appears. Do the following:

I Click a chart type

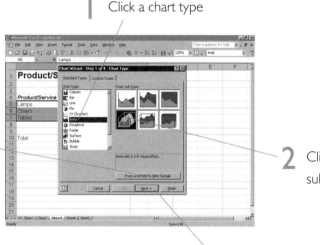

2 Click a chart sub-type

3 Click Next

There are three more dialogs to complete. Carry out the following steps:

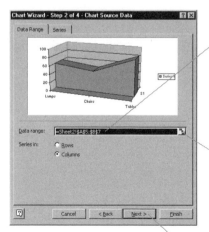

Click here

4 If you selected the wrong cells before launching the Chart Wizard, click here; then carry out the procedures in the HOT TIP

The Collapse Dialog button

5 Click Next

...cont'd

Click any of the additional tabs to set further chart options. For example, activate the Gridlines tab to specify how/where gridlines display. Click Legend to determine where legends (text labels) display. Or click Data Labels for wide-ranging control over the content and formatting of data labels...

You can convert the whole of a 2D chart (or just a data series) to a new type. (With bubble and most 3D charts, though, you can only change the entire chart.)

Select the chart. Pull down the Chart menu and click Chart Type. Now follow steps 1-3 on page 171.

Alternatively, you can apply a custom chart type. Launch the Chart Type dialog (as above). Activate the Custom Types tab. In the Chart type: field, click a custom type. Click OK.

Re step 8 – if you don't want to use the default chart sheet name, you can type in a new one here.

Excel 2002 now launches the third Chart Wizard dialog. Carry out the following additional steps:

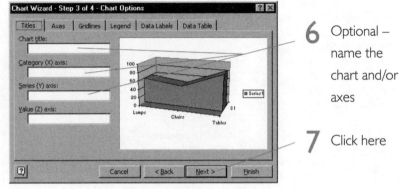

6 Optional – name the chart and/or axes

7 Click here

In the final dialog, you tell Excel whether you want the chart inserted into the current worksheet, or into a new chart sheet.

Carry out step 8 OR 9 below. Finally, perform step 10.

8 Click here to create a chart sheet

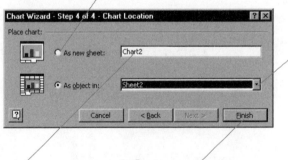

9 Click here; select an existing sheet in the list

10 Click here to generate the chart

172 | Excel 2002 in easy steps

Formatting charts

To add text to a chart, click it. Type in the text; press Enter. Excel 2002 places it near the centre of the chart; drag the text to the correct location.

To amend the formatting of a chart component, do the following:

1 Double-click the frame of the component you want to format

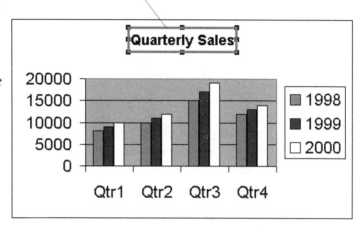

You can rotate text along chart axes. To do this, double-click the text frame e.g.:

Frame

In the dialog, click the Alignment tab. Type in a plus or minus rotation in the Degrees field. (You can also use this dialog to set horizontal and vertical text alignment and text direction.) Click OK.

2 Activate the relevant tab

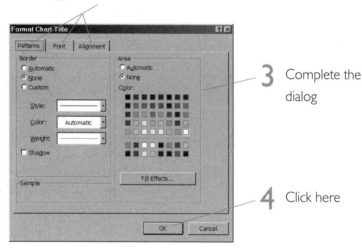

3 Complete the dialog

If you aren't sure what a chart component refers to, move the mouse pointer over it; Excel displays an explanatory Chart Tip e.g.:

Chart Title

4 Click here

Page setup for charts

Most page setup issues for charts in chart sheets are identical to those for worksheet data. The main difference, however, is that the Page Setup dialog has a Chart (rather than a Sheet) tab.

In the Chart tab, you can opt to have the chart

- printed at full size

- scaled to fit the page

- user-defined

You can also set the print quality.

You can specify where on the page an embedded chart prints by moving or resizing it in Page Break View. See page 160.

(See the DON'T FORGET tip below for how to resize chart sheets.)

Using the Chart tab in the Page Setup dialog

Click the relevant chart tab in the worksheet Tab area. Pull down the File menu and click Page Setup. Now carry out step 1 below, followed by steps 2-3 as appropriate. Finally, carry out step 4.

See elsewhere in chapter 14 for detailed advice on how to print worksheets and charts.

Ensure the Chart tab is active

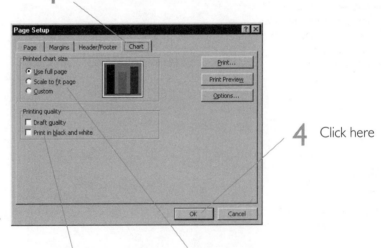

4 Click here

Re step 3 – clicking Custom ensures that, when you return to the chart sheet, the chart size can be adjusted with the mouse in the normal way. The chart then prints at whatever size you set.

2 Click either option here to limit the print quality

3 Click any scale option here (see the DON'T FORGET TIP)

Saving charts to the Web

To publish your charts on the Web, you must have a live Internet connection.

If you publish charts interactively, you may lose some formatting.

You can publish your charts (either as chart sheets, or as charts embedded in worksheets) to the Internet or intranets. This produces HTML files which can be viewed in more or less any browser, without the need to have access to Excel 2002. You can publish charts non-interactively or interactively.

(See page 61 for details of non-interactive v. interactive publishing.)

Publishing interactive charts

Select the relevant chart or chart sheet. Pull down the File menu and do the following:

Refer to (and implement where appropriate) steps 1–7 on page 62 before you carry out the procedures discussed here.

(Pay particular attention to step 1.)

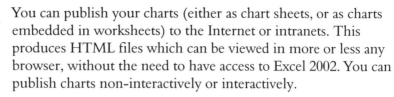

I Click Save as Web Page

If you want to save a chart non-interactively, first select it. Carry out the relevant procedures on page 63 (after step 1, however, ensure that Selection: Chart is activated).

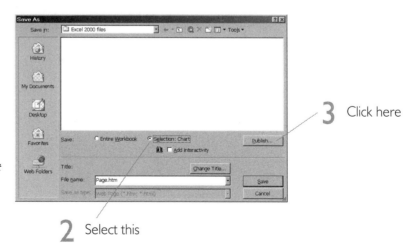

3 Click here

2 Select this

Now carry out the following additional steps:

4 Optional – click here; in the list, select the type of data you want to publish

Tick AutoRepublish every time this workbook is saved to have Excel automatically update your Web file each time you carry out a save operation. (Make sure you select the Refresh option in your browser – e.g. press F5 in I.E. 5.x – when viewing.)

5 Optional – specify a data item

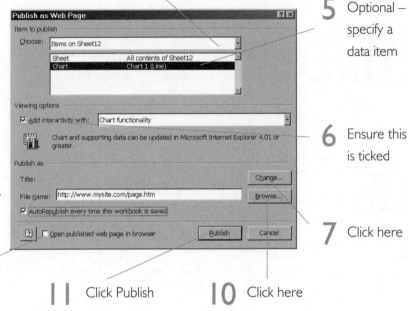

6 Ensure this is ticked

7 Click here

To preview your chart in your browser, select Open published Web page in browser before you carry out step 11.

11 Click Publish

10 Click here

Re step 10 – use the Publish As dialog which now launches to select a destination folder and name the HTML file. (You can use it to save the file to a local network folder or to a Web/FTP folder – see chapter 4.)

Finally, perform step 11.

8 Name the published chart

Set Title

Title:

1st Quarter Results

The title will appear centered over the published selection.

OK   Cancel

9 Click here

Inserting pictures

Inserting pictures via the Insert Clip Art Task Pane

First, position the insertion point at the location within the active worksheet where you want to insert the picture. Pull down the Insert menu and click Picture, Clip Art. Do the following:

Enter one or more keywords

Clips have associated keywords. You can use these to locate clips.

3 Click Search

You can add new clips to collections (or add new keywords to existing clips) in the Clip Organizer. Click here to launch it:

2 Optional – click here and make the appropriate choices

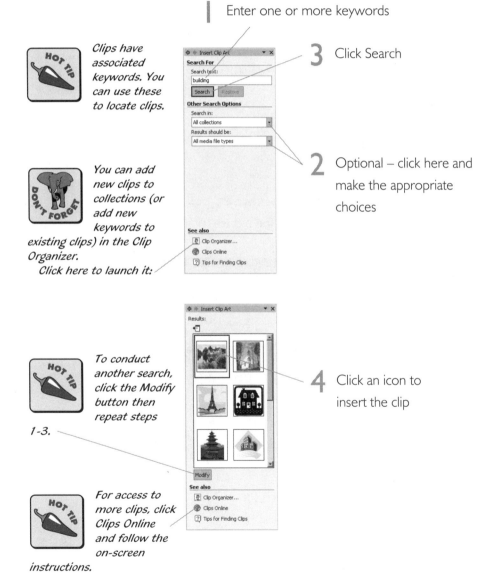

To conduct another search, click the Modify button then repeat steps 1-3.

4 Click an icon to insert the clip

For access to more clips, click Clips Online and follow the on-screen instructions.

Once inserted into a worksheet, pictures can be resized and moved in the normal way.

Inserting pictures – the dialog route

First, position the insertion point at the location within the active worksheet where you want to insert the picture. Pull down the Insert menu and do the following:

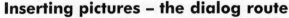
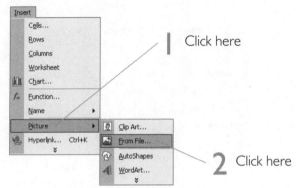

Click here

2 Click here

You can insert pictures onto chart walls. First, select the chart wall then follow the procedures described here.

4 Click here. In the drop-down list, click the drive/folder that hosts the picture

6 Click here

Excel 2002 provides a preview of what the picture will look like when it's been imported – see the Preview box on the right of the dialog.

If this isn't visible, click the following toolbar icon repeatedly until it is:

3 Make sure All Pictures... is showing. If it isn't, click the arrow and select it from the drop-down list

5 Click a picture file

Using AutoShapes

If you want to add text to an AutoShape, right-click it. In the menu, click Add Text. The insertion point appears inside the figure; type in the text. Click outside the AutoShape.

AutoShapes represent an extraordinarily flexible and easy-to-use way to insert a wide variety of shapes into your worksheets. Once inserted, they can be:

- resized

- rotated/flipped

You can also add text to AutoShapes – see the HOT TIPS. Excel 2002 automatically aligns text optimally.

Changes you make to an AutoShape also affect any inserted text.

Inserting an AutoShape

Refer to the Drawing toolbar – if it isn't currently visible, pull down the View menu and click Toolbars, Drawing. Do the following:

To change an AutoShape into another shape, select it. Click the Draw button in the toolbar. In the menu, select Change AutoShape. In the sub-menus, select a new category/shape.

2 Click an AutoShape category

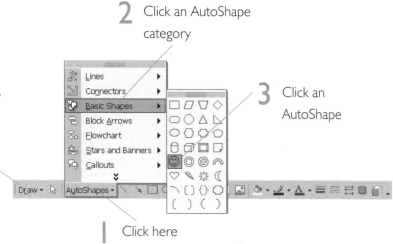

3 Click an AutoShape

Click here

4 Place the mouse pointer where you want your AutoShape to start

Re step 5 – hold down Shift as you drag to maintain the original height/width relationship.

5 Using the left mouse button, drag out the shape

To rotate or flip an AutoShape, select it. Click the Draw button in the toolbar. In the menu, select the relevant option.

You can make some AutoShapes 3D. Select the AutoShape then click this button in the toolbar:

In the menu, select a 3D shape (or No 3-D to restore it to 2D).

A 2D shape converted to 3D

For access to more design elements on the Web, click Clips Online and follow the on-screen instructions:

Resizing AutoShapes

Select the AutoShape. Now do the following:

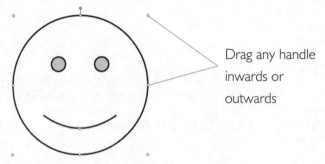

Drag any handle inwards or outwards

Access to more AutoShapes

| To access additional AutoShapes, follow step 1 on page 179. In 2, however, click More AutoShapes

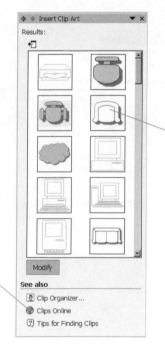

2 Drag an AutoShape into your worksheet

Using macros

Automating frequently performed tasks by recording them as macros can save you a great deal of time and effort.

This chapter shows you how to record tasks as macros and play them back whenever necessary. First, you'll learn how to set your macro security level, to prevent unauthorised macros from running when you open workbooks, then master macro naming conventions.

Finally, you'll go on to associate the macros you create with keystrokes, menu entries, toolbar buttons, graphics and hotspots, so they can be launched with just a few key-presses or mouse clicks.

Covers

Chapter Sixteen

Recording a macro

Excel 2002 lets you automate any task which you undertake frequently. You do this by recording it as a macro. A macro is a recorded series of commands which can be 'rerun' at will. Using macros can save you a considerable amount of time and effort.

Once recorded, macros can be rerun:

- with the use of a special dialog

- by clicking a toolbar button

- by pressing a keystroke combination (defined when you record the macro)

- by clicking a special menu entry

- by clicking buttons, graphics or hotspots

Recording a macro

First, plan out (preferably on paper) the precise sequence of actions involved in the task you want to record. Pull down the Tools menu and do the following:

Click here

2 Click here

...cont'd

Re step 3 – macro names are subject to the following stipulations:

• they must not be the same as cell names

• they must begin with a letter

• after the first letter, you can use letters, numbers and underlines (but not spaces)

Re step 4 – Excel 2002 assumes you want the shortcut key which will launch the macro to be:

Ctrl+?

where ? is any letter.

However, you can also incorporate Shift into any keystroke combination; simply hold down one Shift key as you type in the letter. For example, to have the macro invoked by pressing:

Ctrl+Shift+H

hold down Shift and type in 'h' (minus the quotes).

Macros can't be undone.

Now carry out the following steps:

3 Name the macro

5 Optional – type in extra descriptive text

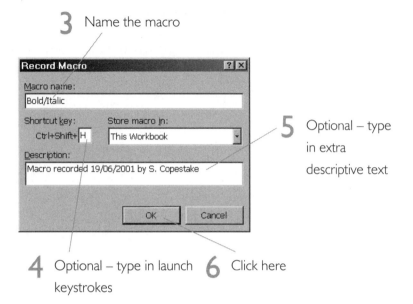

4 Optional – type in launch keystrokes

6 Click here

Perform the actions you want to record. When you've finished, do the following:

The Stop Recording toolbar

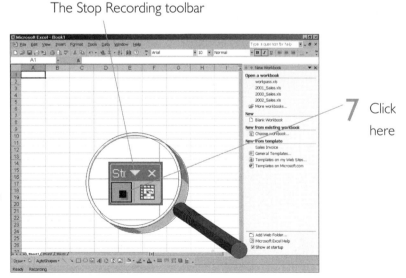

7 Click here

Running a macro

You can run macros in a variety of ways.

The dialog route

First, select the cells you want to apply the macro to. Pull down the Tools menu and carry out the following steps:

You can assign macros to buttons or graphics, so that clicking them starts the macro.

Left-click the button or graphic, then right-click any selection handle. In the menu, select Assign Macro. In the Assign Macro dialog, double-click the relevant macro.

To activate the macro, left-click the button or graphic.

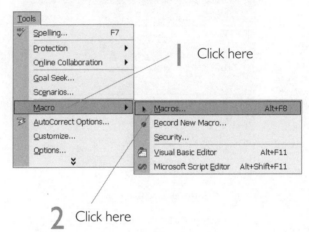

Click here

2 Click here

3 Select a macro

To terminate a macro which is running, press Esc. In the Microsoft Visual Basic dialog, click End.

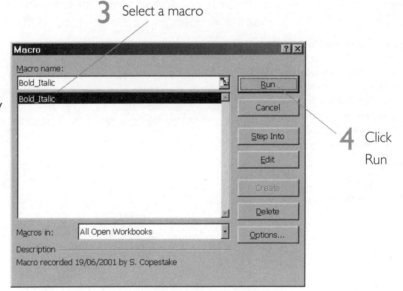

4 Click Run

See the HOT TIP on page 186 for how to impose macros as entries on menus.

You can launch macros via hotspots. To do this, first create an AutoShape for use as a hotspot. With this selected, right-click a selection handle and select Assign Macro. In the Assign Macro dialog, double-click the macro you want to assign to the hotspot. With the graphic still selected, press Ctrl+1. In the Format AutoShape dialog, select the Colors and Lines tab. In the Fill/Color field, select No Fill; in the Line/Color field, select No Line. Click OK.

Now drag the graphic over another larger graphic. Because the fill and line colour are set to none, the first graphic is invisible:

Left-clicking the hidden hotspot (the cursor changes to a pointing hand) launches the associated macro

The menu route

First, select the cells you want to apply the macro to. Pull down the menu to which you've added the macro and do the following:

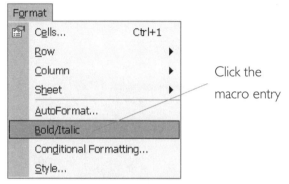

Click the macro entry

The toolbar route

If you've created a special toolbar button and allocated the macro to it (see page 186 for how to do this), select the relevant cell(s) and do the following:

Click here (this is the default macro toolbar icon)

The keystroke route

If you've allocated a keystroke combination to the macro during the creation process (see page 183 for how to do this), select the cell(s) you want to amend and press the relevant keys.

For instance (and to continue the original example from pages 182–183), to italicise and embolden cell contents in one operation, press:

Ctrl+Shift+H

Assigning macros to toolbars

To assign a macro as a new button on a toolbar, first make sure the toolbar is visible (see page 11 for how to do this). Move the mouse pointer over the toolbar and right-click once. In the menu which appears, click Customize. Now do the following:

1 Ensure the Commands tab is active

You can add macros as menu entries. Follow steps 1 and 2. In step 3, drag this button:

Custom Menu Item

onto the menu of your choice. Now right-click the resultant menu entry. In the menu which launches, carry out steps 6–7. Perform step 8 to allocate a macro to the menu entry.

Finally, carry out step 9.

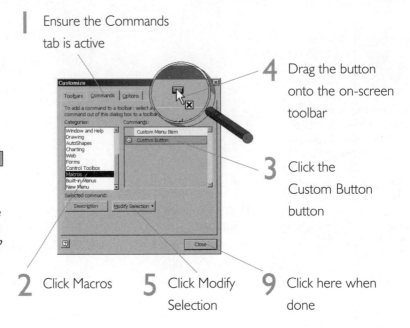

4 Drag the button onto the on-screen toolbar

3 Click the Custom Button button

2 Click Macros

5 Click Modify Selection

9 Click here when done

Re step 6 – ensure you leave in the ampersand – for instance, you could type in:

&Bold_Italic

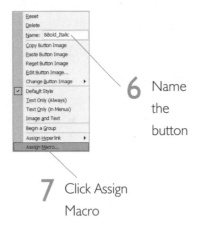

6 Name the button

7 Click Assign Macro

8 Double-click the macro you want to assign to the new button

Index

A

D

E

F

G

H

I

L